Collective Biographies

LEGENDS OF AMERICAN DANCE AND CHOREOGRAPHY

Carin T. Ford

Enslow Publishers, Inc.

40 Industrial Road	PO Box 38
Box 398	Aldershot
Berkeley Heights, NJ 07922	Hants GU12 6BP
USA	UK

http://www.enslow.com

Acknowledgement

The author wishes to extend special thanks to Phil Karg, Photo Specialist with The Dance Collection, a division of the New York Public Library for the Performing Arts, for his help with selecting many of the photographs in this book.

Library of Congress Cataloging-in-Publication Data

Ford, Carin T.
    Legends of American dance and choreography / Carin T. Ford.
        p.   cm. — (Collective biographies)
    Includes bibliographical references (p.) and index.
    Summary: Profiles ten influential and dedicated dancers and choreographers who worked in America, including Martha Graham, Fred Astaire, and Mikhail Baryshnikov.
    ISBN 0-7660-1378-2
    1. Dancers—United States Biography Juvenile literature. 2. Choreographers—United States Biography Juvenile literature. [1. Dancers. 2. Choreographers.] I. Title. II. Series.
    GV1785.A1F64   2000
    792.8'092'273—dc21
    [B]   99-38818
                                                                CIP

Printed in the United States of America

10 9 8 7 6 5 4

To Our Readers:
All Internet addresses in this book were active and appropriate when we went to press. Any comments or suggestions can be sent by e-mail to Comments@enslow.com or to the address on the back cover.

Every effort has been made to locate all copyright holders of material used in this book. If any errors or omissions have occurred, corrections will be made in future editions of this book.

Illustration Credits: Alvin Ailey® American Dance Theater archives, p. 78; ⌐. 54; Kenn Duncan/Alvin Ailey pp. 37, 65, 69. *All other photos in New York Public Library (NYPL) !den Foundations:* pp. 16, 45, 51, PL/Soichi Sunami/pp. 14, 42; ⌐rge Platt Lynes/pp. 26, 31; ⌐ Duncan/p. 80; NYPL/Richard N. Greenhouse/p. 97.

Cover Illustration: Photofest

Contents

Preface 4

1 Martha Graham 7

2 Fred Astaire 17

3 George Balanchine 25

4 Agnes de Mille 35

5 Katherine Dunham 44

6 Jerome Robbins 55

7 Bob Fosse 63

8 Alvin Ailey 71

9 Twyla Tharp 81

10 Mikhail Baryshnikov 91

Glossary 99

Chapter Notes 100

Further Reading 109

Index 111

Preface

"Nobody is born a dancer," ballet star Mikhail Baryshnikov once said. "You have to want it more than anything."[1]

The dancers and choreographers in this book came from different hometowns and experienced vastly different childhoods. Alvin Ailey grew up in Texas, where he picked cotton alongside his mother. George Balanchine stole food during the Russian Revolution to keep from starving. Bob Fosse was an average boy from Chicago except for the secret he kept from his friends: He had been dancing professionally since grade school.

Each dancer's struggle was different. But they shared a common bond—they wanted to dance more than anything.

The people listed here achieved considerable success. The words *legendary* and *greatest* are often used in describing their accomplishments. Did they merely want to dance, or did they want something more? What made Bob Fosse perform routines over and over until he was close to collapsing? What made Agnes de Mille worry about every detail of a dance number until the dancers changed her name from Agnes to "Agonize"? What made Fred Astaire rehearse up to eighteen hours a day, sometimes losing fifteen pounds, before he was satisfied with a single dance routine?

"I wanted to make it good, then make it better," said Astaire.[2]

He was not alone.

Jerome Robbins labeled himself a perfectionist, adding, "I wear that badge proudly."[3] As a child, Twyla Tharp was often told by her father, "I don't care if you dig ditches, as long as you dig the best ditches."[4]

Their accomplishments sprang from raw talent and rawer determination. Yet great achievements in dance are not the sole property of the people included in these pages. Ruth St. Denis, Ted Shawn, Merce Cunningham, Maria Tallchief, Bill "Bojangles" Robinson, Arthur Mitchell, and so many others made tremendous contributions to their art.

The dancers in this book also made great contributions. Then they went a step further. Martha Graham is credited with being the most influential person in the history of modern dance. Katherine Dunham's African-Caribbean rhythms helped form the basis of dance in today's musical theater. Fred Astaire turned dancing on film into an art form. The first woman to direct a Broadway show, Agnes de Mille transformed musical theater by integrating dance and plot. Mikhail Baryshnikov played a major role in boosting Americans' annual attendance at dance concerts from one million in 1965 to more than 15 million in 1975.[5]

These dancers' lives and achievements could be arranged on a time line, marking the year of Graham's first modern dance concert, or the founding of

Balanchine's New York City Ballet. But it would be more accurate to take that line and stand it upright, like a tree, with a strong trunk supporting dozens of branches. No branch survives independently. No tree thrives without the development of new buds.

So it is with dance.

"There was a body that wanted to move around," wrote Tharp of herself. "But it wasn't particularly contented with any of the ways it was presented with. So it went off to find what felt right."[6]

Tharp branched off in a new direction, something she described as "too balletic to be modern, too modern-dance to be ballet."[7] Yet her style was rooted in ballet, jazz, tap, and modern dance.

When de Mille used dance as part of the story in the musical *Oklahoma!*, she was building on Balanchine's work nearly a decade earlier in *On Your Toes*. Jerome Robbins further developed the use of choreography on Broadway with *West Side Story*, a musical where dance and story are not only inseparable but often indistinguishable. Alvin Ailey's masterpiece, *Revelations*, was based partly on his boyhood memories of Texas, but also on the African-Caribbean dances of Dunham. Fosse idolized Astaire; Baryshnikov studied under Balanchine.

The dancers in this book traveled various paths that led them to different and often unexpected destinations. But their origins were the same—they wanted to dance more than anything.

1

Martha Graham
(1894–1991)

Martha Graham's father put a drop of water on a glass slide and asked his young daughter what she saw. Standing on a pile of books to see better, Martha replied that she saw water. "Pure water?" asked Dr. Graham. Martha said yes. He then put the slide under a microscope and asked Martha to look through the lens. She was shocked to discover that the water had wriggling shapes in it. "Yes, it is impure," said Dr. Graham. "Just remember this all of your life, Martha. You must look for the truth."[1]

Known as the mother of American dance, Martha would search for the truth for close to one hundred years.[2] Throughout her long career as a modern dancer and choreographer, she would break rules and shock people in order to find it.

Martha Graham was called a "brilliant young dancer" for her star performance in *Xochitl*, based on American Indian dances.

On May 11, 1894, George and Jane Graham's first daughter, Martha, was born in Allegheny, Pennsylvania. Martha's father was a doctor, and her mother was a descendant of Miles Standish, a Pilgrim on the *Mayflower*. The Grahams later had two more daughters, Mary and Georgia.

When Martha and her sisters were children, they were cared for by Lizzie Prendergast, an Irish woman who loved the theater and often sang to the girls. Martha was not a well-behaved child. When she was two, she sat with her parents during Sunday church services. One day, as the organist began to play, Martha leaped out of her pew and danced down the aisle. Her parents were horrified.[3]

Martha was not taken to the theater as a child, but she used her imagination and created a stage in her bedroom, with a bedsheet for a curtain. Mrs. Graham often sewed costumes for her daughters and supplied them with inexpensive jewelry and scarves.

Mrs. Graham moved with her daughters to Santa Barbara, California, in 1908. The Grahams hoped the climate would improve Mary's asthma, a respiratory ailment. Dr. Graham continued his medical practice in Pennsylvania. He visited his family often and eventually moved to California in 1912.

Martha attended Santa Barbara High School. Although she was small, Martha was athletic and strong, and she played on the girls basketball team. The energy and intensity she gave to the sport would later become her trademark on stage.

When she was seventeen, Martha saw a poster advertising a recital by Ruth St. Denis, a dancer who combined her own freestyle movement with exotic dance. Martha had never seen a dance performance, and she begged her father to take her. When Martha watched St. Denis perform, her life was changed forever.[4] She was determined to become a dancer.

Martha Graham stopped playing basketball and concentrated on drama instead, appearing in local and school productions. After her graduation from high school in 1913, she did not go to an academic college, as her parents wanted. Graham enrolled instead in the Cumnock School, which focused on literature, art, and dramatics. After Graham's first year there, her father died. She was allowed to continue school, although money was scarce.

Ruth St. Denis remained Graham's idol. When Graham learned in 1916 that St. Denis and her husband, Ted Shawn, ran a dance school called Denishawn in Los Angeles, she enrolled in it. Denishawn was a school of the arts and taught its students more than dance. Graham learned how to make costumes, a practice she continued throughout her career. She was also taught yoga, which required her body to be on the floor. Years later, she would choreograph many works where the dancer's body was on the floor.

Most dancers begin their training around age eight, and Graham was already twenty-two. With her short frame and rather plain face, she did not look like a dancer. But she was very determined to succeed and worked harder than anyone else in the school.[5] Shawn noticed Graham's dedication and intensity. Offstage, that intensity came out in violent bursts of temper. When angry, she might rip a telephone off the wall or throw dishes. But Shawn believed Graham would be an electrifying performer onstage.[6]

Shawn created the dance *Xochitl* for Graham in 1920. The work was based on American Indian dances, and Graham danced the title role. She was called "a brilliant, young dancer" by one newspaper critic.[7] Graham became a star performer with *Xochitl.* She was also placed in charge of the entire company when they went on tour. This gave Graham valuable experience for the day when she would run her own company.

Graham left Denishawn in 1923. She was nearly thirty and wanted to strike out on her own. Traveling to New York, she was hired to perform in the Greenwich Village Follies as the leading dancer. Graham performed four solos a night and earned a good salary.

But it was not enough. She left the Follies in 1925. "I wanted to create my own dances, on my own body," she wrote later.[8] Graham was offered a teaching job at the Eastman School of Dance in Rochester, New York. Although Graham was given her own studio and many students, she was still not satisfied. Dance at this time was considered merely a form of entertainment. Graham wanted it to be something more meaningful. She knew that to find what she was looking for, she needed to be completely on her own.

After a year in Rochester, Graham took several students with her and moved to New York City. Louis Horst, who had played the piano at Denishawn, went with her as musical advisor and pianist. For her troupe's first concert, Graham had to borrow $1,000 as well as the Follies theater for the event. Follies producer Morris Green told Graham if the concert failed, she would have to pay him back by performing again in the Follies for one year.

Some dance historians say modern dance began the night of Graham's first concert—April 18, 1926.[9] She had choreographed eighteen short works for the event. At the second intermission, Morris Green went backstage and told Graham, "You made it."[10] She would not go back to performing in the Follies.

Graham had been searching for the truth for years. Now, by dancing her own way, she was getting close to finding it. Instead of pointed toes, Graham's feet were flexed. Instead of leaping into the air, Graham used the floor. Instead of slippers and shoes, Graham had bare feet. Instead of graceful, flowing movements, Graham's choreography was bent and angular.

Graham was using dance to reveal what words could not. She was once asked if it upset her when audiences did not understand her dances. "I am not interested whether they understand or not," Graham said. "I am only interested if they feel it."[11]

Graham launched her own dance company in 1929. It became one of the first major companies to include African-American dancers. Her first important work that year was *Heretic*. Graham, as the lead dancer, tried to break through a human wall that was formed by a group of dancers. She choreographed *Lamentation* in 1930. This famous dance solo was performed entirely on a bench. Graham swayed and leaned, and tried to become the essence of grief. In 1935, her dance *Frontier* depicted life on the American plains.

Graham's company was invited to perform at the 1936 Olympic Games in Berlin. At that time, Germany was ruled by Nazi dictator Adolf Hitler. Graham refused to attend the Olympics because many artists she admired were being persecuted. A year later, she danced at the White House for President Roosevelt and his wife. She would dance for seven presidents in her life.

The most famous of Graham's works is *Appalachian Spring*. Set to the music of American composer Aaron Copland, the 1944 dance tells the joyful story of a pioneer wedding and a young couple resolutely facing the future. Graham danced the lead with Erick Hawkins, who became her husband in 1948. The marriage lasted only a few years, and Hawkins later went on to form his own company.

With bent and angular movements, Graham portrayed the essence
of grief in her dance solo *Lamentation*.

Graham choreographed close to two hundred works in her lifetime. Some were based on Greek myths, such as *Clytemnestra* (1958), *Night Journey* (1947), and *Cave of the Heart* (1946). Graham turned to literature for *Letter to the World* (1940), based on the life of American poet Emily Dickinson, and *Deaths and Entrances* (1943), inspired by the English Brontë sisters.

Graham's dance technique is taught throughout the world today and is based on the new dance vocabulary she created.[12] The technique focuses on the body's true rhythm—breathing. Each exhale is a contraction of the torso muscles; each inhale is a release of the muscles. Dancers such as Twyla Tharp, Paul Taylor, and Merce Cunningham have been heavily influenced by Graham's methods.

Performing until her mid-seventies, Graham won numerous awards for her work. The most notable was the Presidential Medal of Freedom in 1976. She was the first dancer-choreographer to receive this honor.

Graham died on April 1, 1991, at the age of ninety-six. Considered an American genius, she was the first woman in history to create an enormous body of theatrical work that was new and varied.[13] Graham's quest for meaning turned her into a pioneer who established modern dance as an art form. When she was asked in 1975 about the future of dance, Graham answered, "If I knew, I'd do it."[14]

Fred Astaire

Fred Astaire
(1899–1987)

When Frederick Austerlitz was four and a half years old, he boarded a train with his mother and older sister, Adele, and headed for New York City. They were leaving their home in Omaha, Nebraska, for Adele's sake. At six years old, Adele was showing real talent in her dance classes, and her parents felt she could get better training in New York. Fred was just going along for the ride.[1]

After they arrived in New York, Adele was enrolled in a dancing school that had been advertised in a local newspaper. Rather than hire a baby-sitter to take care of Fred, his mother enrolled him as well. Yet in years to come, it was Fred, and not Adele, who would one day be considered the greatest dancer in American history.

Fred was born on May 10, 1899, in Omaha. His father, also named Frederick, had come to this country from Austria four years earlier. Frederick Austerlitz was a good-natured, outgoing man who worked as a salesman for the Storz Brewing Company, which manufactured beer. Fred's mother, Ann Austerlitz, was a native of Omaha and ten years younger than her husband.

The family's decision to move to New York, leaving the father behind, was not an easy one. Frederick Austerlitz had lost his job when the Storz brewery shut down in 1904. The temperance movement, which encouraged people to stop drinking alcohol, was sweeping the country, and the people of Nebraska decided to ban alcoholic beverages from their state. Frederick Austerlitz remained in Omaha, trying to find work to support the family. Ann Austerlitz traveled across the country with the children, looking for a school that might launch Adele's dance career.

She found it in Claude Alvienne's dancing school. Alvienne quickly saw how talented Fred and Adele were and suggested they perform in vaudeville, the theatrical variety shows that were popular at that time. Alvienne created a dance routine in which Fred and Adele dressed up as a bride and groom. They danced up and down an enormous wooden wedding cake. The cake was decorated with electric candles and bells that the children played with their hands and feet.

Fred and Adele performed this act onstage for the first time in 1905 at a theater in Keyport, New Jersey. Years later, Fred said he did not remember being nervous. In fact, the theater was located on a pier, and six-year-old Fred was more interested in fishing than dancing.[2]

Using the last name "Astaire" because their father thought it made a better stage name, Fred and Adele performed successfully. One newspaper critic wrote, "The Astaires are the greatest child act in vaudeville."[3] The children earned $50 for a few days' work and soon were hired to perform in New Jersey, Pennsylvania, and New York for $150 a week. This was a lot of money; skilled workers at that time were earning only about $2 a week. Frederick Austerlitz made the first of many trips to New York to help manage his children's career.

Wherever the Astaires performed, it was Adele who got all the attention. One reviewer wrote, "The girl seems to have talent, but the boy can do nothing."[4] Fred and Adele continued performing the wedding cake act throughout the country for five years. Neither child had ever attended public school. Their mother taught them their academic subjects in between dance lessons and performances.

When Adele reached her teens, she grew three inches taller than Fred. It was awkward dancing with her brother, plus she seemed too old for the childish act. The children retired from performing and moved to Weehawken, New Jersey, where they attended school for the first time.

Within two years, Fred grew to Adele's height and the children were enrolled in Ned Wayburn's dancing school. They returned to the vaudeville circuit, and by 1914, both were getting rave reviews. Their act, now shaped by Aurelia Coccia, a successful vaudeville showman, was filled with the latest popular songs.

The Astaires became one of the best-known dance teams in the country. Adele enjoyed their fame, but it only made Fred work harder. "Just practice, sweat, rehearsal and worry" was his formula for success.[5] Throughout his life, Fred would be known as a perfectionist. "I'm cold-blooded about dancing," he once said. "I wanted to make it good, then make it better."[6]

In 1917, the Astaires made their first appearance in a Broadway musical, *Over the Top*. By 1932, Fred and Adele had appeared in ten Broadway shows, including *Lady, Be Good!*, *Funny Face*, and *The Band Wagon*. They also performed in London, where audiences adored them.

The Astaires were now celebrities, but Fred was extremely shy and often stammered during interviews. Adele, who had her father's outgoing personality, enjoyed the attention and fell in love while performing in London. In 1932, she married Charles Cavendish, the second son of the Duke of Devonshire, and she retired from show business.

Fred Astaire was unsure of how to continue his career without his sister. He worried that he would always be known as Adele's little brother.[7] Astaire appeared in one more musical on stage, then decided to try performing in movies. In 1933, he married Phyllis Livingston Potter and flew to Hollywood after a one-day honeymoon.

Astaire did not expect to be successful in the movies. He had always considered himself "a funny looking guy."[8] A studio executive also had doubts, commenting on Astaire's screen test, "Can't act . . . can't sing . . . balding . . . can dance a little."[9]

But Astaire was given a small role in *Dancing Lady*, starring Joan Crawford, and then a larger part in *Flying Down to Rio* with Ginger Rogers in 1933. This was his first Hollywood musical with Rogers, who would be his dancing partner in ten films. Astaire was not happy about being part of a new team; it had been hard enough going out on his own after Adele retired. In a letter to his agent, Astaire wrote, "I did not go into pictures to be *teamed* with her [Rogers] or anyone else."[10] But such films as *The Gay Divorcee*, *Roberta*, and *Top Hat* were very successful, with Astaire's singing voice proving to be very pleasant. Astaire and Rogers became a legendary dance partnership.

One reason for the popularity of the Astaire-Rogers musicals was that the country was in the middle of the Great Depression. It was a time when many people were out of work and had little money.

Movie audiences loved the dance team of Fred Astaire and Ginger Rogers.

Astaire's movies were lighthearted and fun, and they helped people forget their troubles.

Another reason for their success was the dancing. Astaire's vaudeville days had taught him that audiences like a good show. He choreographed routines where he danced with golf clubs, firecrackers, and hat racks, and he often danced on chairs, tables, even ceilings! Astaire's style was unique—an elegant combination of ballroom, tap, and ballet—and he made dancing on film a new art form.[11] His flawless technique and casual grace masked the difficulty of the routines he performed.

Astaire worked hard to make his dancing appear natural and effortless. He often rehearsed up to eighteen hours a day for several weeks, sometimes losing fifteen pounds before he was satisfied with a dance routine. His partners rehearsed with him, and by day's end, their shoes were often caked with blood.[12]

During this time, Astaire and his wife had two children: Fred Junior, born in 1941, and Ava, who was born the following year. Astaire opened the first of a chain of dancing schools across the country in 1947. Two years later, he made his last movie with Rogers, *The Barkleys of Broadway*. He continued appearing in films with other dance partners, such as Audrey Hepburn, Rita Hayworth, and Cyd Charisse.

Astaire's wife died in 1954. By this time, the Hollywood musical was not as popular with audiences, and Astaire turned to television. He hosted and performed on numerous shows and made four musical specials of his own between 1958 and 1968. *An Evening with Fred Astaire* won nine Emmy awards in 1958.

Astaire was sixty-nine when he performed his last dancing role on film in *Finian's Rainbow*. He also tried some serious acting roles in movies such as *On the Beach*, *The Towering Inferno*, and *Ghost Story*.

Astaire received many awards during his lifetime. He received an honorary Oscar in 1949 for his work in film. In 1978, he was one of the first performers to receive the Kennedy Center Honors for lifetime achievement. Three years later, he was given a Lifetime Achievement Award by the American Film Institute.

Astaire had worked in Hollywood for thirty-five years, making more than thirty films. In every movie, Astaire insisted the camera always show his entire body when he was dancing. He would not allow close-ups of his feet or his face. Nothing was to interfere with the flow of the dance and nothing should look faked.[13]

After being a widower for twenty-six years, Astaire married Robyn Smith, a successful jockey, in 1980. She was thirty-five years old and shared Astaire's interest in horses.

When Astaire died on June 22, 1987, President Reagan declared that he was "an American legend."[14] Most members of the dance community considered him the greatest dancer in the world. But as Astaire liked to say, "I just dance."[15]

3

George Balanchine
(1904–1983)

"As a human being, you cannot know in advance what will be best for you."[1]

George Balanchine frequently spoke those words. During his nearly eighty years, he experienced terrible hardship as well as incredible success. A patient man who never raised his voice, Balanchine calmly followed the twists and turns of his life, becoming the most influential ballet choreographer of the twentieth century.[2]

Georgi Melitonovich Balanchivadze was born on January 22, 1904, in St. Petersburg, Russia. He would be known by this name for twenty years until he shortened it to make it easier to pronounce. George's parents were Meliton Balanchivadze, a composer, and Maria Balanchivadze, a talented pianist.

George Balanchine

He had an older sister, Tamara, and a younger brother, Andrei.

George grew up in a rural area outside St. Petersburg. When he was five, his mother started giving him piano lessons. Although he hated practicing, George learned to play extremely well and often played duets with his mother.

At the age of nine, George traveled to St. Petersburg with his mother and sister. He was going to be enrolled in the Imperial Naval Academy. Some of his relatives had careers in the Navy, and George was pleased with the idea. But the academy had already selected its cadets for the year, and there was no room for George.

Disappointed, George's mother brought him along for his sister Tamara's audition at the Imperial School's ballet academy. It was hoped that Tamara would one day become a famous ballerina. A school official suggested that George audition as well. The young boy walked in front of the judges, who saw that he was strong and had good posture. George was accepted into the school; Tamara was not.

George was not happy about being left at the school, and he ran away. His aunt who lived in St. Petersburg brought him back. The first year was hard. George hated the long hours of ballet exercises and did poorly in all his subjects, except music and religion. He was not liked by the other students, who called him "Rat" because he would sniff and show his teeth.[3] The one joy in George's school life was playing the piano. Word soon spread that George was the best pianist at the Imperial School, even though he was one of the youngest.

George's attitude toward dance changed when he was asked to appear with several other students in the Imperial Ballet Company's performance of *Sleeping Beauty*. George enjoyed being onstage, and he now realized the importance of the rigorous ballet exercises he performed every day.

In 1917, the Russian Revolution broke out. The revolutionaries took over the government and overthrew the royal family, and the Communists seized control of the country. The Russian Empire became the Soviet Union. George's school was shut down. After a brief stay with his family, George was sent back to St. Petersburg to live with his aunt in case the school reopened. He never saw his parents or his sister again.

During this turbulent time, there was little to eat and occasionally George risked his life stealing food for himself and his aunt. At fourteen, he held various jobs, including playing the piano in an old movie theater. He would often be paid not in money but with flour, rice, or honey.[4]

The ballet school reopened in 1918. Two years later, George created his first ballet, *La Nuit*. "I loved music and suddenly I wanted to move people to music, to arrange dances," he said years later.[5] School officials liked the piece, and George continued choreographing dances until he graduated with honors in 1921.

George Balanchine became a dancer with the State Academic Theater of Opera and Ballet. But he also enrolled in the Petrograd Conservatory of Music and even considered becoming a composer. The musical training Balanchine received would make him stand out among other choreographers in years to come. Typically, choreographers believed that dance steps are more important than the music. But Balanchine always felt dance and music should be woven together.

On July 4, 1924, Balanchine left the Soviet Union. He traveled with a few other dancers to Germany, France, and England, looking for places to perform. The Soviet government soon ordered him home, but Balanchine did not return. Living conditions there were terrible. But more important, he wanted the freedom to experiment with his choreography, which he was unable to do in the Soviet Union.

Serge Diaghilev, who ran the Ballets Russes dance company in Paris, had seen some of Balanchine's work and hired him as choreographer. The Ballets Russes was the most famous dance company in the world at the time. With powerful music and exciting dancing, it set new trends in dance.[6] The most famous ballets Balanchine created for the company were *Apollo* (1928) and *Prodigal Son* (1929). Balanchine worked for the Ballets Russes from 1925 until Diaghilev's death in 1929. "It is because of

Diaghilev that I am whatever I am today," Balanchine said years later.[7]

By this time, Balanchine was known as one of the most exciting choreographers in Europe. He was out of work, but Balanchine was not a man who worried about the future. He remained calm and patient over the next four years, working for such companies as the Paris Opera, the Royal Danish Ballet, and his own company, Les Ballets 1933, which folded after one year.

When Balanchine was twenty-nine, he met Lincoln Kirstein, who was on a trip to Europe. Kirstein was a wealthy American who wanted the United States to have a major ballet company. Kirstein asked Balanchine to come to the United States and help develop ballet in America. At that time, there was no place for an American dancer to perform ballet except in musical theater.[8] Balanchine's first priority was to start a school. Eventually, the two men would form the New York City Ballet.

The School of American Ballet opened on January 1, 1934. Six months later, the students danced in *Serenade*, the first ballet Balanchine had choreographed in the United States. In *Serenade*, Balanchine emphasized a group, or ensemble, of dancers rather than focusing on an individual dancer. He did this because he never knew who would show up each day at his school. The ballet typified Balanchine's style: no plot, and continuous movement by the dancers.

George Balanchine instructs a group of youngsters in ballet.

It took Balanchine and Kirstein fourteen years to actually form the New York City Ballet. Their first company, called American Ballet, lasted only from 1935 to 1938. During that time, it became the ballet company of the Metropolitan Opera, with Balanchine at its head. Although Balanchine choreographed more than twenty-three operas there, his fresh style of dance clashed with the traditional opera productions. The ballet company left the opera, and without financial support, it folded.

While his dance school continued, Balanchine worked on Broadway. He choreographed eighteen musicals, including *On Your Toes* (1936), which contained the famous *Slaughter on Tenth Avenue* ballet. Balanchine's work on Broadway was groundbreaking.[9] Dance was used for the first time as part of the plot instead of as a separate act. In years to come, choreographers Agnes de Mille and Jerome Robbins would further develop the idea of integrating dance, songs, and story in musical theater. Balanchine was also the first to request that the word *choreography* be used when giving credit to the person who created the show's dances.[10]

Balanchine choreographed the film version of *On Your Toes* in 1939 along with four other movies. In 1942, he even choreographed a work for Ringling Brothers Circus, using fifty elephants!

Still hoping to put together their own company, Balanchine and Kirstein formed the Ballet Society in 1946. Two years later, it became the New York City

Ballet. Balanchine worked with the dancers to develop a new kind of ballet with the emphasis on speed and precise movements. To focus the audience's attention on the dancing and music, he kept the scenery simple and modified the practice leotards to use as costumes. Under Balanchine's artistic direction, the company became one of the greatest in the world.[11]

By the 1960s, the New York City Ballet was putting on one hundred fifty performances a year. Always interested in music, Balanchine turned to a variety of composers to accompany his choreography. He created *Divertimento No. 15* (1956) to the music of Mozart, *Stars and Stripes* (1958) to John Philip Sousa's music, and *Who Cares?* (1970) to George Gershwin's.

Through the years, Balanchine often worked with Russian composer Igor Stravinsky to create some of the century's greatest ballets. Stravinsky believed Balanchine's musical ability enabled him to turn rhythm, melody, and harmony into the visual patterns of dance.[12] Some of Balanchine's ballets set to Stravinsky's music include *Orpheus* (1947), *The Firebird* (1949), and *Agon* (1957).

Balanchine's life had often been difficult. He had known starvation, he had lost a lung in his twenties after being seriously ill with tuberculosis, and he had frequently been without work. He also had four failed marriages to ballerinas—Tamara Geva, Vera Zorina, Maria Tallchief, and Tanaquil LeClerq. But

Balanchine never panicked or lost his temper. Only hours before the premiere of *The Nutcracker* in 1954, Balanchine learned that the costumes were not ready. Without a word, he picked up a needle and calmly began working with the seamstresses. "There sat Balanchine, sewing away as if he didn't have a care in the world," said choreographer Jerome Robbins.[13]

Balanchine died April 30, 1983. Nearly a year after his death, it was discovered that he had died from a rare virus that causes Creutzfeldt-Jakob disease, a fatal brain infection.

Balanchine created more than two hundred major ballets and was one of the first artists to receive the Kennedy Center Honors for lifetime achievement. A gifted teacher and showman, Balanchine is regarded as one of the greatest choreographers in the history of ballet.[14]

Agnes de Mille
(1905–1993)

Agnes de Mille stood onstage, bowing to a cheering audience after dancing the lead role in her ballet *Rodeo*. It was October 1942, and de Mille was sure the performance had been terrible. Even when the musicians in the orchestra stood up to applaud, de Mille believed the evening had been a failure in what often seemed a lifetime of failures.[1] Finally, her dance partner nudged her and said, "This is an ovation. This is the real thing. Take it."[2] Twenty-two curtain calls later, de Mille believed it.

At the age of thirty-seven, after years of hard work and determination, she had finally succeeded as a choreographer.

On September 18, 1905, William and Anna de Mille's first child, Agnes, was born into a theatrical family in Harlem, New York. William de Mille was a writer for both the stage and screen, and his brother, Cecil B. De Mille, was a famous Hollywood film director.

Agnes grew up spending the school year in New York City with her younger sister, Margaret. Summers were spent at Merriewold, a country estate at the foot of the Catskill Mountains in Sullivan County, New York. Agnes spent much of her time roaming through the woods at Merriewold, observing the birds, deer, and raccoons and playing with two imaginary forest friends, Gockle and Dickie.

A stream of guests visited the de Milles at Merriewold, including actors, writers, and musicians. "We lived on music," Agnes wrote of those summers.[3] It was here that Agnes started piano lessons at the age of five, later claiming she learned to read music before she could read words.[4]

When Agnes was nine, her father began writing screenplays for movies—which were silent in those days—and the family moved to Hollywood, California. Agnes was allowed to visit the movie sets while her Uncle Cecil was shooting films. She often dressed up like the actresses and would even attach spools of thread to her shoes to imitate high heels.

Agnes used the garage at home to construct castles, inns, and theaters. She prayed each night that her parents would let her act in the movies. Agnes got her chance when she was ten and appeared in *The*

Agnes de Mille dances the lead role in her ballet *Rodeo*, set in the American West.

Ragamuffin, a film written by her father. She earned $5 for a day's work.

Agnes had asked for dance lessons from the time she was five, but her parents refused. In the early 1900s, dance was not considered a suitable activity for a proper young lady. Agnes learned as much as she could about dance by reading and keeping a scrapbook of dancers' photographs. When she was thirteen, Agnes saw a performance by Anna Pavlova, the great Russian ballerina. This made her even more resolved not only to study dance, but to become a dancer. "I was as clearly marked as though she had looked me in the face and called my name," Agnes wrote about seeing Pavlova perform.[5]

At last, when a doctor suggested ballet lessons to strengthen Margaret's feet, Agnes's parents gave both daughters permission to study dance. Although Agnes had finally gotten her wish, she was already a young teenager, a late time of life to start dancing. She also did not possess the lean body of a dancer. She worked hard at her lessons, even though she considered herself the worst pupil in the class.[6]

William de Mille never really approved of his daughters' dancing. In an effort to please him, Agnes stopped taking lessons when she was seventeen. She enrolled at the University of California at Los Angeles as an English major. Studying a variety of subjects, Agnes de Mille graduated in 1926 with honors. But what she really wanted to do was dance.

De Mille's parents separated after her graduation. Unable to stay away from dance, de Mille moved with her mother to New York, where she began looking for work as a dancer and choreographer. She quickly realized she was not qualified. "I had never so much as bought a hat without my mother's advice," she wrote.[7] No one would hire her, but she did not give up. De Mille debuted as a choreographer in 1927 when she performed her work *Stage Fright.* It told the story of a dancer nervously warming up before a recital.

Her mother rented theaters so de Mille would have a place to perform such works as *Ouled Nail* and *May Day.* Drawing on her years in Hollywood, de Mille told stories with her dances and used colorful costumes and props. She was determined to succeed and once even continued performing when another dancer accidentally kicked her and broke her nose in the middle of a concert.

In 1932, de Mille was hired to do the choreography for a new Broadway show called *Flying Colors.* Lacking experience, she made many mistakes and was eventually fired.

De Mille left New York and moved to Europe, where she performed her own dances and was occasionally hired as a choreographer. In 1938, she returned to the United States. She was thirty-three years old with no money and no job. De Mille considered abandoning her dance career and working as a salesclerk at Macy's.

Before she could apply for a job at the department store, de Mille was asked if she had an American dance that could be performed by the Russian dance troupe the Ballet Russe de Monte Carlo. "I didn't," she said later. "But I lied and I said, 'Certainly, I'll go home and get it.' So I went home and wrote it."[8]

The result was *Rodeo*, an American ballet set in the West with music by American composer Aaron Copland. Playing the lead role of Cowgirl, de Mille taught the dancers how to walk like cowboys, squint in the sunlight, and dance as if they were riding horses. She worried about every gesture, causing some dancers to change her name from Agnes to "Agonize."[9]

"If it is possible for a life to change at one given moment," de Mille wrote about the opening night of *Rodeo*, ". . . then my hour struck at 9:40, October 16, 1942. Chewing gum, squinting under a Texas hat, I turned to face what I had been preparing for the whole of my life."[10] Rodeo was an instant success, and it marked de Mille as an important American choreographer.

The following year, the songwriting team of Richard Rodgers and Oscar Hammerstein II asked de Mille to choreograph a musical that also had to do with cowboys and horses—*Oklahoma!* Previously, dance in a musical usually was used either to fill time during scenery changes or simply to display pretty dancers on stage. But de Mille tried something new with her choreography. She combined ballet, modern dance, and folk dance to develop the characters and help tell the story. She choreographed quickly to get the dance numbers ready for opening night. Occasionally, she lost her temper and had to be "held under a faucet of cold water until I quieted down," she wrote.[11]

When *Oklahoma!* opened at New York's St. James Theatre in March 1943, some of the dancers were injured and others had contracted the German measles. But the show was a hit, and de Mille's choreography changed American musical theater forever. Dance would no longer be used as a sideshow. It became an important part of the entire production, and it was de Mille who made *ballet* a household word for millions of Americans.[12]

Three months after the opening of *Oklahoma!*, de Mille married Walter F. Prude, a concert manager from Texas. De Mille had been introduced to Prude by her friend Martha Graham, the modern dance choreographer. Because of World War II, Prude was in the Army, and the couple spent little time together for the next two years.

But de Mille kept busy. The success of *Oklahoma!* ensured that she would never again struggle to find work. She choreographed musicals such as *One Touch of Venus* and *Carousel,* and the ballet *Tally-Ho.* When the war ended in 1945, de Mille was at work on the musical *Brigadoon.* She also directed the shows *Allegro* and *Out of This World.*

De Mille, left, used colorful costumes and props to tell stories in her dances, such as this scene from *May Day*.

De Mille gave birth to a son, Jonathan de Mille Prude, on April 20, 1946. By this time, de Mille had decided she wanted to be known as more than a Broadway choreographer.[13] She wrote a serious ballet called *Fall River Legend* for Ballet Theatre, the company that would later become American Ballet Theatre. It told the story of Lizzie Borden, who was accused of hacking her parents to death with an ax in 1892. The 1948 ballet has become a classic.

De Mille returned to choreographing musicals as well as writing books. Her fourteen volumes include several memoirs as well as books about dance. In 1975, de Mille suffered a stroke, leaving her paralyzed on her right side. She was not expected to survive, but de Mille refused to give up. She lived by two words: "I will."[14] She relearned how to walk, resumed choreographing, and eventually even performed again.

De Mille won numerous awards for her contributions to the world of dance, including the National Medal of the Arts in 1986. Her lectures and television programs helped educate the public about dance.

On October 7, 1993, de Mille died of another stroke. She had asked only to be remembered as a dancer. Yet it was her choreography that transformed American musical theater and helped popularize ballet in America.

5

Katherine Dunham
(1909–   )

Katherine Dunham was supposed to stay in the apartment with the door locked. Only three years old and too young for school, she had lived with relatives since the death of her mother. Katherine was often left alone, but on this particular day, she unlocked the front door and wandered into the hallway. She heard voices singing and followed the sound.

In the basement, she saw her Aunt Clara and cousin Irene dressed in costumes and wearing stage makeup. They were rehearsing a musical show, *Minnehaha*, which they hoped to perform in a theater. Katherine huddled unseen in a corner, fascinated by the singing and colorful clothing.

The incident stayed with her over the years. It "may have inspired in some small way my own

Katherine Dunham

eventual choice of a theatrical career," she wrote.[1] Theater would play an important part in the life of Katherine Dunham, noted dancer, anthropologist, writer, teacher, and the first African-American choreographer to be known throughout the world.[2]

Katherine Dunham was born on June 22, 1909, in Glen Ellyn, Illinois, outside Chicago. Her parents were Albert Dunham, a salesman, and Fanny June Dunham. Katherine was close to her older brother, Albert Jr., and also had five grown half-brothers and half-sisters from her mother's first marriage.

When Katherine was three, her mother died. Katherine and Albert Jr. were sent to live with their Aunt Lulu in a poor section of Chicago. Aunt Lulu was a beautician and unable to care for Katherine during the day. She decided Katherine should attend school. Since there was no kindergarten, Lulu added a year and a half to Katherine's age and enrolled her in first grade.[3] But Katherine was frightened at school and lost her way walking home. After three days, Katherine was taken out of school.

While Aunt Lulu worked, Katherine was watched by either her brother—who had to miss school in order to baby-sit—or her cousin Irene. Irene loved the theater and used the money Lulu left for food and coal to buy tickets to the vaudeville shows. Katherine would spend the day on her cousin's lap, sometimes sleeping, sometimes watching the performances of the singers and dancers onstage.

Katherine's half-sister Fanny June Weir arrived at the apartment one day and took Katherine and Albert Jr. back to her own home. Although Fanny Weir lived in a more comfortable neighborhood than Lulu and provided the children with plenty of food and heat, Katherine and her brother did not feel welcome and they were unhappy.[4]

When Katherine was five, her father brought the children to Joliet, Illinois, to live with him and his new wife, Annette Poindexter. Katherine attended Beale School, where she received good grades in reading, writing, spelling, music, and physical education; she received bad grades in arithmetic. Her behavior was also poor. Katherine often talked when the students were supposed to be studying, and rather than walk directly to class, she would dreamily take her time.[5]

Katherine did not particularly like school, but she enjoyed playing sports and excelled as an athlete. She also had fun forming a secret society, "The Eagle Eye." Katherine made red satin headbands with beads, which the club members wore until the principal banned them.

Katherine went on to attend Farragut Elementary School and Joliet High School, where she participated in hockey, basketball, and the dance club. Katherine also took ballet lessons, which was something few African-American children could afford at the time. Katherine enjoyed her lessons and was an excellent dance student.[6]

After she graduated from high school, Katherine was encouraged by her brother to attend the University of Chicago. He was working toward a degree in philosophy there. Eighteen-year-old Katherine Dunham traveled to Chicago to attend classes at the university. She continued dance lessons in tap and ballet, and became interested in starting her own dance school.

With the help of two ballet dancers from the Chicago Opera Company, Dunham began the Ballet Negre in 1930. The African-American ballet troupe performed at the Chicago Beaux Arts Ball in 1931 but soon ran out of money and had to disband. Dunham attempted to start two more dance schools. Neither was successful, partly because many African Americans at that time were not teaching their children about their heritage. "Negro mothers refused to send their children to me, for fear they might be taught Negro dancing," she said.[7]

In 1934, dancer and choreographer Ruth Page asked Dunham to dance the solo lead in *La Guiablesse*. It is based on a folktale from the island of Martinique in the West Indies. Dunham performed at the Chicago Opera's theater, and as a result of her work, she was selected to train a group of dancers for the 1934 Chicago World's Fair. She formed a company of seven dancers, and their performance was well received.

At the University of Chicago, Dunham became interested in anthropology—the study of human origins, development, and behavior. Anthropology professor Robert Redfield lectured about the importance of dance on culture.

Dunham was aware that African Americans had a special style of dance.[8] She also knew there were few opportunities for African-American dancers in the 1930s. Dunham decided to research the dances of African cultures and to explore the role that dance plays in society.

Supported by a grant from the Rosenwald Foundation, Dunham traveled to several Caribbean islands in 1935. She studied such dances as Martinique's martial arts dance, *L'Ag'Ya*, and the West Indian *mazouk*. In Jamaica, she participated in the sacred war dance of the Koromantees, a tribe that originally came from the West Coast of Africa.

"The songs are in lusty Koromantee, and from somewhere a woman procured a rattle and is shaking it . . . ," Dunham wrote of the war dance. "Some of the men wave sticks in the air, and the women tear off their handkerchiefs and wave them on high as they dance."[9]

In Haiti, Dunham found that the people celebrated nearly all their social events with some kind of rhythmic movement. Dunham participated in various festivities, including crowd dances that lasted for days and covered many miles. Dunham was also initiated by secret ritual into the *Vaudun*, or voodoo cult, which required her to walk barefoot over hot coals and to lie on her side for three days with her head wrapped in chicken feathers, almond syrup, and fruit.

Dunham returned to the United States after eighteen months. She formed a new dance company and presented what she had learned about African-Caribbean rhythms. Dunham's first important work was *L'Ag'Ya* (1938), based on the Martinique dance. Typical of Dunham's dances, *L'Ag'Ya* has colorful costumes and scenery and is a high-energy performance.

In 1941, Dunham married John Pratt, who designed her productions for the next forty-five years. They adopted a daughter, Marie Christine, in 1951.

Audiences enjoyed Dunham's performances and were surprised to find African-American dances being offered as culture. Choreographer Agnes de Mille wrote: "Dunham's contribution is like no other, and oddly enough, it is the one true historical contribution of her people to American dance."[10]

Traveling to New York in 1939, Dunham's dance troupe performed the shows *Le Jazz "Hot"* and *Tropics* on Broadway. When choreographer George Balanchine saw one of her performances, he asked Dunham and her dancers to appear in the Broadway show *Cabin in the Sky* (1940). After going on tour with the show, the Katherine Dunham Dancers made their way to Hollywood and appeared in the films *Star-Spangled Rhythm* (1942) and *Stormy Weather* (1943).

Katherine Dunham's dances are high-energy performances with fancy, colorful costumes.

The dances that Dunham created as a result of her Caribbean studies have helped form the basis of dance in today's musical theater.[11] Between 1938 and 1965, Dunham choreographed 150 ballets, six Broadway and European shows, three operas, and thirteen films.

Wherever Dunham traveled with her dance company, she refused to tolerate discrimination against African Americans. In 1944, after performing in front of a segregated audience in Lexington, Kentucky, she told the audience, "This is the last time we shall play Lexington, because the management refuses to let people like us sit by people like you."[12] In 1952, a hotel in Brazil would not allow Dunham to enter. She filed a lawsuit that led to the outlawing of discrimination in public places by the Brazilian legislature.

By 1963, Dunham was focusing her attention on establishing a performing arts training center in the ghetto of East St. Louis, Illinois. One of her goals was to turn young people away from crime and drugs by encouraging them to attend classes in ballet, martial arts, foreign languages, photography, music, and wood carving. Among her students was Jackie Joyner-Kersee, who later became a famous Olympic athlete. "Our people came from the streets," Dunham said. "I wanted to offer a rational alternative."[13]

Throughout her life, Dunham has continued to fight for human rights. In 1992, she fasted for forty-seven days to draw attention to the United States' treatment of Haitian refugees. She finally ended her hunger strike at the urging of former Haitian president Jean-Bertrand Aristide.[14]

Dunham has been called a living legend. She ran one of the first African-American dance companies, and her dance techniques are now part of nearly every jazz dance class that is taught.[15] Through her work as a dancer and choreographer, Dunham has waged a constant battle against race discrimination. Her awards include the Kennedy Center Honors for lifetime achievement and the National Medal of the Arts.

"I used to want the words 'She tried' on my tombstone," said Dunham. "Now I want 'She did it.'"[16]

Jerome Robbins

Jerome Robbins
(1918–1998)

By the time he was a teenager, Jerome Robbins knew he wanted to be a dancer. His parents, however, believed dancing was for girls. They argued at length with their son to choose any career—even making shoes—other than dancing.[1]

"They sent me to every relative they could find, saying, 'Don't do it,'" Robbins remembered. "But I wanted to do it."[2]

Robbins's determination, combined with his hard work and originality, made him the first major American-born choreographer of ballet. He also left a permanent imprint on Broadway's musical theater.

Harry and Lena Rabinowitz's second child, Jerome, was born in New York City on October 11, 1918. Harry Rabinowitz, who ran a delicatessen, and

Lena Rabinowitz, a homemaker, came to the United States to escape persecution in Russia and Poland. When Jerome was very young, his father began working in the corset industry and the family moved to Weehawken, New Jersey.

Harry and Lena Rabinowitz believed in offering Jerome and his older sister, Sonia, as many cultural opportunities as possible.[3] Jerome took piano lessons and performed in a public children's concert when he was only three. Throughout his youth, he also played the violin, learned how to paint, and accompanied his sister to dance lessons.

Jerome graduated from high school in 1935 and applied for a scholarship to the School of American Ballet, run by the famous choreographer George Balanchine. His application was turned down, but Robbins later believed it was for the best.

"Sometimes I ponder the idea of what would have happened when I was seventeen years old if the school had said, 'Yes, come here,' and I had become a Balanchinite before I found my own voice," he said. "I tend to feel that because Balanchine was such a giant of a choreographer, I was happy to have come to my first works on my own."[4]

Jerome Robbins attended New York University as a chemistry major for one year. He had to drop out because his father's business was doing poorly and money was scarce. Robbins took dance classes with his sister's modern dance teachers, Gluck Sandor and

Felicia Sorel. Occasionally he had to scrub floors to pay for the lessons.[5]

Gluck Sandor worked with various theatrical companies. Through him, Robbins made his first professional debut. He had a two-word part in the Yiddish Art Theater's 1937 production of *The Brothers Ashkenazi*. Sandor also taught Robbins the importance of relating to the audience. When Robbins later became a successful choreographer of musical theater and ballet, one of his greatest gifts would be his storytelling ability, which drew the audience into the action onstage.[6]

During the mid-1930s, Robbins spent his summers working on the entertainment staff of Camp Tamiment, a Poconos resort hotel in Bushkill, Pennsylvania. At the camp, Robbins sang and danced in shows and even began choreographing on his own. His dance version of Thornton Wilder's play *Our Town* was used in *The Straw Hat Revue*, which was performed in New York in 1939.

The dance training Robbins received through the years was diverse. In addition to modern dance, he studied ballet, Spanish dance, and Asian dance techniques. There were very few permanent dance companies in the United States at this time, and Robbins found himself drawn to the musical theater of Broadway. Here, he danced in the chorus of four musicals, including *Great Lady* (1938) and *Keep Off the Grass* (1939).

In 1940, the Ballet Theatre—later called American Ballet Theatre—was founded, and Robbins became a dancer with the company. He studied with such choreographers as Eugene Loring, known for his ballet *Billy the Kid,* and English choreographer Antony Tudor. Robbins was made a soloist after one year and danced the title role in the ballet *Petrushka* in 1943.

Robbins's success as a dancer allowed him to try his hand at choreographing and performing a work of his own.[7] He was twenty-five when he created *Fancy Free,* a groundbreaking work that is generally considered among his finest ballets.[8] It tells the story of three sailors—one of whom was played by Robbins—on shore leave in New York during World War II.

As in many of Robbins's works, *Fancy Free* presented a slice of American life. Ballet in the United States had previously rested in the hands of foreign-born choreographers and dancers. In *Fancy Free,* Robbins combined an American story with the contemporary American music of composer Leonard Bernstein. He also blended classical ballet with American popular dance. Nothing like it had ever been seen before. At its premiere, *Fancy Free* received twenty-five curtain calls and Robbins became an overnight star.[9]

The ballet was so successful that eight months later, Robbins and Bernstein expanded the work into a musical, *On the Town.* The show opened December 28, 1944, and was an instant hit. For the next twenty

Robbins, center, became an overnight star in *Fancy Free*, his ballet about three sailors.

years, Robbins would frequently cross the line between classical dance and Broadway, winning four Tony awards for such shows as *High Button Shoes* (1947), *The King and I* (1951), *Peter Pan* (1954), *Bells Are Ringing* (1956), *West Side Story* (1957), *Gypsy* (1959), and *A Funny Thing Happened on the Way to the Forum* (1962). His last musical, *Fiddler on the Roof* (1964), ran for 3,242 performances and was his most commercially successful work.

In 1948, Robbins joined Balanchine's New York City Ballet as a dancer, choreographer, and eventually associate artistic director. He retired from dancing at age thirty-four and devoted himself to choreography.

Two of the better-known ballets that he created for the New York City Ballet were *The Cage* (1951) and *Afternoon of a Faun* (1953). While Balanchine's ballets often contained no plot, Robbins's works usually told a story or described a situation. In *Afternoon of a Faun*, a boy and girl stared at themselves in an imaginary mirror while they rehearsed. *The Cage* depicted man-eating insects.

Robbins once explained how he created a dance: "As I go along, I seem to start to get a sense of what [a piece] is about. Sometimes I'm very surprised by where I begin and end up. That's why I can't understand how people can say, 'Oh, I do the ending first.' I can't do that. I have to get to it by the logic of what the choreography leads to."[10]

Moving easily between the worlds of ballet and Broadway as no other choreographer had done, Robbins conceived, directed, and choreographed the musical *West Side Story* in 1957. Set to Bernstein's music, the show was an updated version of William Shakespeare's play *Romeo and Juliet*, with Robbins pitting two New York gangs—the Jets and the Sharks—against each other.

West Side Story was the first show to be built around the choreography, instead of having the traditional emphasis on story and songs.[11] From the opening scene where gang members snap their fingers as they walk rhythmically through the streets, dance and movement are inseparable in the show.

Admitting that he was a perfectionist, Robbins was often hard to work with. He attended to every detail of *West Side Story*, which won ten Oscars in the film version. "I know I'm difficult," he told the show's cast. "I know I'm going to hurt your feelings. But that's the way I am."[12] He even separated the two "gangs" of dancers throughout rehearsals to create an atmosphere of tension when they finally performed together on stage.

"When Robbins takes over a show, it's his vision in every department. He drives the set designer crazy, he drives the orchestrator crazy, he has a total vision of what he wants," said Sheldon Harnick, lyricist for *Fiddler on the Roof.* "He presses you and presses you on every point, no matter how trivial, until it isn't trivial any more."[13]

Robbins continued working on Broadway even after he left the New York City Ballet in 1958. He also began his own company, Ballets: U.S.A. Although the troupe was popular in Europe, it did not do well in the United States and folded in 1962.

Robbins choreographed *Les Noces* for Ballet Theatre in 1965 and then received a three-year grant from the National Endowment for the Arts. He experimented with different theater techniques in his American Theater Laboratory, but no public performances came out of the project.

In 1969, Robbins returned to the New York City Ballet, where he was named ballet master by Balanchine. *Dances at a Gathering* (1969) and *The Goldberg Variations* (1971) are two important works he created. When Balanchine died in 1983, Robbins and dancer Peter Martins became artistic directors of the company.

Robbins continued choreographing through 1997. His last ballet was *Brandenburg*, a piece set to the Bach concertos. He suffered a stroke and died July 29, 1998, at his home in New York City.

Working to eliminate the boundaries between classical ballet and popular dance, Robbins choreographed sixty-six ballets and fifteen shows in his lifetime. Above all, he wanted his dancing to seem a natural part of human behavior.[14] According to Adolph Green, who wrote the book and lyrics for *On the Town*, "Things that might at first seem ordinary, he made it seem that you had never seen them before."[15]

Bob Fosse
(1927–1987)

At the age of twelve, Bob Fosse was leading a double life. During the day, he seemed like any other boy at Ravenswood Grade School in Chicago, Illinois. He was athletic, popular, a good student, and a big fan of the Chicago Cubs baseball team. But after school, Bob did something he rarely mentioned to his friends: He danced. This love of dance and the theater would stay with Bob throughout his life, and his unique, jazzy style of dance would eventually make him one of Broadway's leading choreographers.

One of six children, Robert Louis Fosse was born on June 23, 1927, in Chicago. His father, Cyril Fosse, had once performed in vaudeville. His mother, Sara Fosse, played the piano and loved the theater.

When Bob's older sister, Patricia, was ten, she was enrolled in the Chicago Academy of Theatre Arts. She was a tall, shy girl and sobbed at the thought of attending dance school. Eight-year-old Bob was sent along to keep Patricia company.

Bob became hooked on dance lessons from the start. School director Frederic Weaver loved vaudeville and made sure his students were trained in tap, ballet, acrobatic dancing, and drama. Even as a child, Bob had his own way of doing things. He was taught to hold his arms out wide when he danced, but Bob tucked in his elbows. He was told to keep his fingers together, but he spread them apart.

Although Bob enjoyed dancing, taking lessons presented problems. His brothers often poked fun at him for carrying tights in his schoolbag. Also, Bob's small size made him an easy target for bullies. He once said he carried chocolate candies to hand out to the bigger boys who wanted to beat him up.[1]

But he continued with lessons, and soon Weaver teamed Bob with another student about the same age, Charles Grass. Taking the name the Riff Brothers, the boys were performing a tap dance routine in vaudeville theaters before Bob even graduated from elementary school.

In 1941, Bob entered Roald Amundsen Senior High School. He competed on the swim and track teams, received good grades, had numerous girlfriends, and was president of his graduating class. He

Bob Fosse

also spent most weekends performing in nightclubs, theaters, and rowdy dance halls throughout Chicago.

"He was completely absorbed in his dancing," said high school friend Bill Mazer. "Bob and I used to skip school, take the elevated train and go to theaters like the Oriental and the Chicago to see Bill 'Bojangles' Robinson or Paul Draper. . . . We'd stay there all day, mesmerized, and later Bob'd go back home and try to imitate his steps. He always rehearsed alone."[2]

When Bob Fosse graduated from high school in 1945, he knew two things: He wanted to be a professional dancer, and he wanted to enlist in the Navy. He spent nine weeks in boot camp and then joined the entertainment branch of the Navy. Fosse wrote and performed in a show called *Tough Situation,* which toured across the Pacific from Guam to Tokyo. A fellow officer remembered how driven Fosse was to dance, often performing long hours in the heat until he was close to collapsing.[3]

Fosse left the Navy in 1946 and headed for New York to find work dancing in a Broadway show. He was still in uniform when he auditioned for the musical *Call Me Mister.* Dancing for a solid forty-five minutes, Fosse landed the part of the dance lead in the show's national touring company.

The cast of *Call Me Mister* traveled along the East Coast and on to Fosse's hometown of Chicago. His picture appeared in the local newspaper, and most of his high school friends, along with former partner

Charles Grass, came to see him perform. In 1947, Fosse married Mary Ann Niles, a dancer in the show.

When *Call Me Mister* closed, Fosse and Niles found work dancing on stage and in television. In 1950, they appeared in the Broadway show *Dance Me a Song*, where Fosse met dancer Joan McCracken. Fosse and Niles soon divorced, and he married Joan McCracken.

McCracken encouraged Fosse to be a choreographer. In 1951, he created a dance routine for a television show starring actors Dean Martin and Jerry Lewis. McCracken also urged Fosse to go to school. He studied acting, singing, ballet, modern dance, and choreography with Anna Sokolow and José Limón, both modern dance choreographers. That same year, Fosse played the lead in a summer stock production of the musical *Pal Joey*.

Fosse went to Hollywood in 1952 to appear in the movie *Give a Girl a Break*. Nearby, dancer Fred Astaire—Fosse's idol—was making a film. Fosse loved to watch Astaire rehearse. Once, Fosse saw Astaire kick a nail and send it flying directly into a nearby wall. Fosse practiced kicking a nail for hours afterward until he was able to do the same thing.[4]

Fosse danced in the movie *Kiss Me Kate* before being hired to choreograph his first Broadway musical, *The Pajama Game*. Only twenty-six, Fosse had been recommended for the job by the dancer and choreographer Jerome Robbins. *The Pajama Game* opened in 1954, establishing Fosse as a leading Broadway choreographer and winning him the Tony award for choreography. "It isn't surprising that Fosse's style was there at the very start," said Jerome Robbins. "Either you have a statement to make, and you make it, or you don't. He had a quality that was Bob Fosse's quality and nobody else's."[5]

"Steam Heat," a dance in the show, is possibly Fosse's most famous number. It makes full use of Fosse's trademark style, which he said was based on his own shortcomings as a dancer. Because his own knees and toes turned in, so did his dancers'. When he began losing his hair and took to wearing hats, so did his dancers. Even Fosse's hunched shoulders were reflected in his dancers' postures.[6]

Fosse headed back to Hollywood in 1955 to choreograph and star in the film musical *My Sister Eileen*. He quickly returned to Broadway to create dances for *Damn Yankees* and won another Tony award for choreography.

Fosse worked on eight musicals over the next decade, including *Bells Are Ringing* (1956), *New Girl in Town* (1957), *Redhead* (1959), and *Sweet Charity* (1966). He kept up this hectic pace throughout his life, becoming both choreographer and director of his shows. Fosse enjoyed the reputation of being hardworking, hard driving, passionate, and ruthless.[7] "I was always happiest working," he said. "I frequently got bored with other aspects of life."[8] After getting another divorce, he married his third wife, dancer Gwen Verdon, in 1960. Three years later, the couple had a daughter, Nicole.

In 1973, Fosse did something no one had ever done before. He won the major awards in every area of entertainment—two Tony awards for the Broadway show *Pippin,* an Oscar for the film *Cabaret,* and an Emmy for the television show *Liza With a Z,* starring Liza Minnelli.

In 1974, rehearsals had begun for the show *Chicago* when Fosse suffered a heart attack and had to undergo bypass surgery. He told of the experience in the film *All That Jazz* (1980). Based on Fosse's life, the movie tells of a choreographer who smokes too

Fosse directed the movie version of his Broadway hit *Sweet Charity.* In this famous scene, Paula Kelly, left, Shirley MacLaine, center, and Chita Rivera dance on a Manhattan rooftop.

much, abuses drugs and alcohol, works too hard, and devotes his life to dance.[9]

After the heart attack, doctors talked to Fosse about changing his habits and living a healthier life. Still, Fosse continued smoking and drinking and working on shows. *Chicago* opened in 1975, followed three years later by *Dancin'*, Fosse's biggest financial success on stage. In 1986, he worked on his last show, *Big Deal.*

"He's sensational," said dancer Gene Kelly of Fosse's choreography throughout the years. "What they say not to do, he does. He blends different styles, using them where they should be used, and in that way he has practically developed a style of his own."[10]

Fosse traveled to Washington, D.C., in 1987 to get ready for the opening of a revival of *Sweet Charity*. After a morning of rehearsal, Fosse died of another heart attack on September 23.

He left his unique mark on numerous musicals and films. Even people who had never heard Fosse's name recognized his jazzy style of dance with the slouched back, indifferent attitude, and white gloves that called attention to the spread fingers.[11]

"There's something about trying to create something that gives people pleasure . . . maybe somebody will remember you," Fosse once said. "Maybe somebody will say, 'He was a good showman; he gave us good shows. You could always count on him for an evening's entertainment.'"[12]

8

Alvin Ailey
(1931–1989)

It had never occurred to young Alvin Ailey to become a dancer. He did enjoy imitating the dance routines he saw performed by movie stars Fred Astaire and Gene Kelly. But there were few opportunities for African-American dancers in the 1940s. Given Alvin's talent for languages, it seemed most likely he would grow up to be a teacher or a translator.[1]

Alvin's life changed when he was in high school. He visited the Biltmore Theater in downtown Los Angeles, California, and saw Katherine Dunham and her African-American dance troupe perform the show *Tropical Revue.*

"I was lifted up into another realm," he later wrote. "I couldn't believe there were black people on a legitimate stage in downtown Los Angeles, before

Alvin Ailey

largely white audiences, being appreciated for their artistry."[2]

Dunham's company performed at the Biltmore for three weeks—and for most of that time, Alvin sat in the theater watching them. One day, he would create his own dances, merging African-American traditions with the techniques of ballet, jazz, and modern dance.[3]

Alvin Ailey, Jr., was born on January 5, 1931, in Rogers, Texas, about fifty miles south of Waco. His mother, Lula, was seventeen at the time, and his father, Alvin Ailey, abandoned the family when baby Alvin was six months old. To earn money for herself and her son, Lula took any work she could find, including washing, ironing, cleaning houses, and picking cotton.

"My mother was off working the cotton field all day," Alvin wrote years later. "When I was very young, only about four or five, I also picked cotton. . . . When we left the cotton fields at sunset, I would sit on one of the wagons and ride home. I remember the people moving in the twilight back to their little shacks."[4]

When he was six, Alvin moved with his mother to Navasota, Texas. He was a good and quiet student in school, where his chubby build earned him the nickname "Big Head."[5] During these years, Alvin spent his spare time sketching on a large pad he carried with him, playing the tuba, and writing poetry. The town's social life revolved around the Truevine

Baptist Church and a bar called the Dew Drop Inn. In later years, Alvin would base some dances on his memories of these places.[6]

In 1942, Alvin moved to Los Angeles, California, where his mother hoped to find better-paying work. Alvin attended George Washington Carver Junior High School. He sang in the glee club, read for hours in the school library, and showed a strong talent for languages. He also frequently went to the movies and would act out the stories for his mother after he returned home.

When Alvin entered Thomas Jefferson High School in 1945, his class was taken on a field trip to see a Russian dance troupe, the Ballet Russe de Monte Carlo. It was the first time Alvin had seen a dance concert, and he began to spend much of his time in theaters. After watching Katherine Dunham's company perform, the idea of becoming a dancer started to take hold.

Alvin graduated from high school in 1948 and took a dance class taught by Thelma Robinson, who danced in Dunham's company. The class focused on African-Caribbean dances, but Alvin was interested in other styles of dance as well.

"One day," Alvin said, "a friend showed me some movements from a class he was taking, and I nearly fainted. I said, 'Oh, my God, what is that?' And he said, 'That's modern dancing.'"[7]

Friend and future colleague Carmen de Lavallade took Alvin Ailey to see a performance by Lester

Horton, the modern dance choreographer. Despite his self-consciousness about his lack of training and large size, Ailey began taking classes with Horton, whom he considered the greatest influence on his life.[8] Ailey spent five years as one of Horton's students and performers in his company, periodically attending the University of California at Los Angeles and San Francisco State College to study languages. When Horton died of a heart attack in 1953, Ailey took over as the dance company's director.

Ailey began creating his own work. *According to St. Francis* and *Morning Mourning* premiered in June of 1954. Later that year, Ailey flew with de Lavallade to New York to perform in the Broadway musical *House of Flowers.* The show lasted only a few months, but Ailey remained in New York and began studying modern dance with Martha Graham, Hanya Holm, and Charles Weidman. He also studied ballet with Karel Shook and took acting lessons from Stella Adler, a well-known teacher. Out of work, and with little money or food, Ailey broadened his knowledge of the theater by attending the numerous music and dance concerts in New York.

Over the next two years, Ailey landed some roles as a dancer and actor. He performed in the film *Carmen Jones,* on the television show *The Amos and Andy Musical Hall,* and in the off-Broadway play *The Carefree Tree.*

In 1957, Ailey performed as a lead dancer in the musical *Jamaica.* But more important, he was allowed to use the theater to rehearse some new dances he was working on. "I very much wanted to be a choreographer," he wrote. "I had wearied of doing other people's concerts. . . . I was tired of being told what to do. I had my own ideas, and the time had come for me to make my own decisions."[9]

Ailey put on his first concert on March 30, 1958, at the Ninety-second Street Y in New York City, and the Alvin Ailey American Dance Theater was launched. The works performed at his first concert included "Redonda (Five Dances on Latin Themes)," "Ode and Homage," and "Blues Suite," a piece based on Ailey's memories of the Dew Drop Inn and Truevine Baptist Church in Texas.

From the beginning, Ailey had a vision for his company. He wanted to show "that color is not important, that what is important is . . . a culture in which the young are not afraid to take chances and can hold onto their values and self-esteem."[10]

Ailey choreographed twenty new ballets during his company's first decade. One of his best-known works is *Revelations* (1960), celebrating gospel music, spirituals, and small-town religion. It is considered a modern dance classic and made Ailey's troupe one of the major companies in modern dance.[11] Ailey was also interested in the origins of modern dance. He revived works by modern dance pioneers Ted Shawn and Katherine Dunham.

In 1962, Ailey's company went on a tour of Southeast Asia as part of the President's Special

International Program for Cultural Presentations. Ailey's group quickly became the most popular dance company on the international touring circuit, performing works on six continents.

In the United States and abroad, Ailey's company attracted large numbers of people, many of whom had never before been exposed to dance. He succeeded by making his dances fun to watch, with high-energy performances, flashy costumes, varied music, and elaborate sets.

Occasionally, the performances were criticized for being too theatrical. "The black pieces we do that come from blues, spirituals and gospels are part of what I am," Ailey said. "If it's art *and* entertainment—thank God, that's what I want it to be."[12]

Ailey stopped dancing in 1965 so he could concentrate on choreography. He created seventy-nine ballets during his lifetime, as well as choreographing such works as Leonard Bernstein's *Mass* and the opera *Anthony and Cleopatra* by Samuel Barber. Many of Ailey's works have been performed by the American Ballet Theatre, the Joffrey Ballet, the Dance Theater of Harlem, and the Paris Opera Ballet.

Although Ailey's company was composed solely of African-American dancers for the first six years, the troupe became integrated in 1964. Ailey wanted dancers of all races to communicate the joys, sorrows, and hopes of African Americans. "I felt that people were people and that a black theme expressed by

Alvin Ailey, above, created dances that were both interesting and fun to watch. He said that he wanted his dances to be "art *and* entertainment."

dancers of all colors would be enlarged," he said. "It became a universal statement."[13]

His awards include the Samuel H. Scripps American Dance Festival Award for lifetime contribution to modern dance in 1987 and the Kennedy Center Honors for lifetime achievement in 1988.

Newspapers across the country reported Alvin Ailey's death on December 1, 1989, of a rare blood disorder. He is remembered as a dancer, choreographer, teacher, and, most important, a man who introduced millions of people to African-American culture and traditions through dance.

Today, his company continues to flourish under the direction of Judith Jamison, who had been one of Ailey's star dancers and the inspiration for his well-known solo "Cry."

"He made dance accessible to everyone," said former Ailey dancer Keith McDaniel. "You didn't have to have a trained eye or read a book—all you had to do was open your heart. That's what Alvin was all about, that spark of spirit."[14]

Twyla Tharp

9

Twyla Tharp
(1941–)

Twyla Tharp was eager to read the newspaper on May 1, 1965. The night before, she had danced in the first work she had ever created, "Tank Dive." The dance lasted only seven minutes and included a yo-yo, a subway pole, various angular body positions and no music.

She hurried to the newsstand, practically holding her breath as she searched for the reviews of her performance. She was afraid that "not only would I embarrass myself as a choreographer but the critics and the audience would say I wasn't even good enough to be a real dancer."[1]

Tharp checked *The New York Times* and the *New York Post* and did not find any bad reviews. In fact, she did not find *any* reviews. "I couldn't believe the critics didn't realize what we had here was history created last night," she said later.[2] It would be several years before critics would take notice of Twyla Tharp, but eventually they would recognize her as a major choreographer in the world of dance.

Twyla was born on July 1, 1941, on a Portland, Indiana, farm.[3] She was the first of Lecile and William Tharp's four children. Twyla was destined for stardom since the moment of her birth. Her mother wrote on the birth announcement, "She'll grow up to be famous."[4] She named her daughter Twyla after the reigning local "Pig Princess," substituting a *y* for the original *i* because she thought it would look better on a theater marquee. Lecile Tharp gave piano lessons and often played music by composers ranging from Mozart and Bach to George Gershwin and Fats Waller. William Tharp, Twyla's father, owned a car dealership.

Lecile Tharp did everything she could to make sure her daughter would be famous. When Twyla was only one and a half, her mother began training her ear by teaching her the different notes and chords on the piano. Twyla began taking piano lessons when she was four.

In 1949, the Tharps moved from their farm to Rialto, California, about one hundred miles from Hollywood. William and Lecile Tharp had built a drive-in theater, which they planned to run. Twyla spent a lot of time at the theater, usually eating her dinner there—Coke syrup, candy corn, red hots, ice cream bonbons, and popcorn.

Running the theater did not distract Lecile Tharp from her daughter's education. She found teachers from as far as one hundred miles away to train Twyla in ballet, baton, flamenco dancing, drums, violin, viola, painting, acrobatics, shorthand, German, and French.

Both of Twyla's parents made it clear they expected their daughter to excel. "I don't care if you dig ditches, as long as you dig the best ditches," her father often said.[5] Twyla threw a tantrum in the first grade when an A-minus appeared among all the A's on her report card. If Twyla ever scored lower than an A-minus, her mother assumed the teacher was incompetent and removed her daughter from the class and often from the school. Between third grade and high school graduation, Twyla attended seven different schools.

Twyla took her first dance lessons at the Vera Lynn School of Dance in San Bernardino, California. She learned tap, toe, acrobatics, Hawaiian dance, and rope twirling with tapping. By the time she was twelve, Twyla was being driven two hundred miles round trip twice a week to Beatrice Collenette's dance school. She spent countless hours after school in the car and frequently used the light of the glove compartment to do her homework.

Twyla's daily schedule when she was twelve was filled from 6 A.M. until bedtime.

6:00–6:15: put practice clothes on
6:15–7:15: Ballet
7:15–8:00: Violin
8:00–8:30: get dressed, clear room, breakfast
8:30–9:00: go to school
9:00–3:00 (P.M.): go to school
3:00–3:15: go to Mr. Windows
3:15–4:00: Violin lesson
4:00–4:30: come home, snack, practice clothes
4:30–5: 00: Baton
5:00–5:30: Tap
5:30–6:00: Baton
6:00–7:00: kids Ballet (go to show once a month)
7:00–7:30: kids Baton
7:30–8:00: kids Tap
8:00–9:00: homework, shorthand
9:00–9:30: eat supper, get ready for bed[6]

Throughout high school, whenever she was free from music or dance lessons, Twyla liked to read. She read everything from *Popular Mechanics* to Shakespeare to the Bible. On weekends and every night in the summer, she worked at the drive-in. She prepared the hot dogs, waited on customers, and sold tickets. More important, she was able to observe what audiences enjoyed watching and what bored them.

During her teenage years, Twyla began experimenting with the basic dance movements. She would try variations on the traditional exercises she had been taught, such as lifting her leg one way while her torso turned another way.

She attended Barnard College in New York City, majoring in art history. But Tharp found time to take classes in ballet, modern dance, and jazz. Throughout her career, she would stress the importance of learning different styles of dance.[7] She also attended performances of works by such varied choreographers as Martha Graham, Jerome Robbins, Alvin Ailey, Merce Cunningham, and Paul Taylor.

"Watching each, I asked myself one question over and over: 'Is this how I should be dancing?'" she later wrote.[8]

In 1962, Tharp married her college boyfriend Peter Young. She skipped her college graduation the following year and instead went to a rehearsal with modern dance choreographer Paul Taylor. From this rehearsal came Tharp's first dance role. She performed in *Scudorama*, crawling like a crab across the stage with a beach towel draped over her.

But Tharp needed to find her own style of dance, and she left Taylor's company in 1964. "There was a body that wanted to move around," she said of herself. "But it wasn't particularly contented with any of the ways it was presented with. So it went off to find what felt right."[9]

Tharp's marriage to Young ended, and she focused on giving her first concert as a choreographer. She presented *Tank Dive* at Hunter College on April 29, 1965. Her work over the next few years was offbeat and had an aggressive quality; she did not care whether or not the audience enjoyed her dances.[10]

Most dance critics wrote that Tharp's work was bad . . . but interesting.

She married again, this time to Bob Huot, a painter who designed many of her costumes. That marriage also did not last, but they had a son, Jesse, in 1970. At this time, Tharp choreographed *The Fugue*, a work based on twenty twenty-second movements. Performed in silence except for the amplified sound of the dancers' feet hitting the stage, *The Fugue* has been called a masterpiece.[11]

Tharp created her first big success, *Eight Jelly Rolls*, the following year. Using music for the first time, Tharp combined dance with comedy and set it to the early jazz music of Jelly Roll Morton. Tharp used jazz again in *The Bix Pieces* (1971), performed to Bix Beiderbecke's 1920s music, and she combined Scott Joplin's ragtime with Mozart's music in *The Raggedy Dances* (1972).

Her popularity steadily increasing, Tharp created a dance for the Joffrey Ballet in 1973 that merged ballet with the contemporary social dance of teenagers. *Deuce Coupe* was performed to the songs of the Beach Boys and had scenery inspired by New York City's subway-car graffiti.

Tharp's biggest success came in 1976 when she choreographed *Push Comes to Shove* for ballet star Mikhail Baryshnikov. The work switched musical styles from ragtime to classical and also changed dance styles. It was an instant hit.[12]

Twyla Tharp, above, choreographs dances with a loose-jointed, off-balance look.

By the late 1990s, Tharp had already created about one hundred dances. Typically, a Tharp dance has at least two things going on at the same time, and the dancers themselves have a loose-jointed, off-balance look.[13] When she begins creating a work, Tharp often has no idea how it will end up. "At some point in the piece, I begin to feel which movements belong and which don't," she said.[14]

She has choreographed four films: *Hair* (1978), *Ragtime* (1980), *Amadeus* (1984), and *White Nights* (1985). Tharp created a work on ice for Olympic gold-medal skater John Curry. She has choreographed works especially for television, including one piece that compared and contrasted the movements of ballet dancer Peter Martins with football player Lynn Swann. Some of Tharp's works reflect her feelings about life in America, such as *When We Were Very Young* (1980) and *The Catherine Wheel* (1981). She also directed and choreographed the Broadway adaptation of *Singin' in the Rain* (1985).

The American Ballet Theatre honored Tharp in 1984 by presenting an evening of her work. In 1987, Tharp formed Twyla Tharp Dance, a company that focused on classical ballet. After the company folded, she accepted appointments as choreographer for American Ballet Theatre, the British Royal Ballet, and the Paris Opera Ballet.

By 1996, she was back with a company of her own, called Tharp! "I was feeling restrained by the conditions that are required when you work with professional companies," she said. "They have rules. Audiences have expectations. I began to want to make material addressing none of this."[15] The Tharp! company danced some of her old works—including *The Fugue*—as well as her new ones.

With a style Tharp has called "too balletic to be modern, too modern-dance to be ballet," she has drawn on various dance forms for her works: classical ballet, jazz, rock-and-roll, social dancing, acrobatics, tap, and modern dance.[16] But no matter what form it takes, Tharp's work is always full of surprises and has led to her being considered one of the leading choreographers in the world.[17]

"Like counterpoint and harmony in music, there are rules in creating dance," she has said. "They work. They need to get tested, need to get broken."[18]

Mikhail Baryshnikov

10

Mikhail Baryshnikov
(1948–   )

On June 29, 1974, in Toronto, Canada, Mikhail Baryshnikov danced as a guest star in the ballet *Don Quixote* with a famed Soviet company, the Bolshoi Ballet. After the performance, Baryshnikov removed his costume and makeup as usual. He left the theater by the stage door, pushing past the fans who surrounded him.

A few blocks away, a car was waiting to take Baryshnikov away from the dance troupe and away from his Soviet homeland and its Communist government. Baryshnikov was going to defect: He would live permanently in the West, where he could travel freely and make his own decisions about his dance career. As his fans swarmed around him that night, Baryshnikov began to run. The fans ran, too. They were running for autographs, but Baryshnikov was running for his life and the freedom to live it as he chose.[1]

Mikhail Nikolayevich Baryshnikov was born on January 27, 1948, in Riga, Latvia, located in the western part of what was then the Soviet Union. His father, Nikolai Baryshnikov, was a high-ranking army officer, and his mother, Alexandra, loved dance and often took her son to see the ballet.

Misha, as Mikhail was called, was an active child who found it difficult to sit still in school. He participated in many activities, including gymnastics, soccer, fencing, swimming, and folk dancing. But Misha was not a very good student, and he often cheated and lied to get out of doing homework.[2] Outside school, he took piano lessons and also sang in a children's choir. When he thought about his future, Misha imagined becoming a concert pianist and performing onstage with a big orchestra.

At the age of twelve, Misha was enrolled in the School of Opera and Ballet Theater in Riga. He liked the theatrical atmosphere of the school immediately.[3] In his first year, Misha was placed in a beginner's ballet class. His day was divided among rigorous dance classes, academic studies, and piano, music, and fencing.

Misha was short and stocky, which is not the ideal body for a dancer. "Someone told us that tomato juice was good for making you grow tall," remembered Alexander Godunov, a dancer and classmate of

Misha's. "Somebody else told us that sleeping on soft beds would prevent us from reaching our full height. So Misha and I drank tomato juice all the time and took the soft mattresses off our beds and slept on hard boards."[4]

Misha's body may not have been perfect, but he showed a great deal of strength, energy, and motivation. "As a teenager, I knew that whatever I was to become I wanted to be very good at," Misha said. "Nobody is born a dancer; you have to want it more than anything."[5] By age fourteen, he was transferred to an advanced dance class.

During this time, Misha's mother died and his grandmother took care of him. Misha's days were focused on his dance classes. Even as a teenager, he was showing extraordinary ability. "He was perfect in everything that he did," said Bella Kovarskaya, one of Misha's teachers.[6] He danced his first solo at age fifteen in *Tarantella* in a role she created just for him.

In 1964, Misha left his home and traveled to Leningrad to study at the Kirov Ballet's Agrippina Vaganova Leningrad Choreographic Institute. His ballet teacher was the famed ballet master Alexander Pushkin. "It was during the years I studied with this extraordinary man that my basic ideas on dancing and work took shape," Misha said. "Everything he gave me is in one way or another the beginning—the solid beginning—of how I now understand it all."[7]

For the next three years, Misha worked and studied more than twelve hours a day, six days a week. In addition to academic subjects, Misha also took classes in ballet, acting, mime, makeup, and music. When he was seventeen, Misha competed in an international ballet competition in Varna, Bulgaria. It was his first trip outside the Soviet Union. He was only a student, but Misha won the gold medal.

A year later, Mikhail Baryshnikov graduated from the Vaganova school and became a member of the Kirov Ballet Company. Typically, dancers entering the company spent several years in the *corps de ballet*— a group of dancers who perform together. Yet Baryshnikov was a soloist from the start and made his first appearance as a professional dancer in *Giselle* in 1967.

Many of the Kirov dancers were jealous that Baryshnikov danced as a soloist, and they teased him about his short height of five feet seven inches.[8] But Baryshnikov's outstanding technique, especially his ability to jump in the air and hang there as if frozen, put an end to the teasing. By 1969, he was considered a star of the Kirov Ballet. He won another gold medal that year in the first International Ballet Competition in Moscow.

Baryshnikov traveled to England and Holland in 1970. It was his first tour of the West, and he found these countries very different from the Soviet Union. He bought blue jeans and saw shows such as *West Side Story*, *Fiddler on the Roof*, and *Jesus Christ Superstar*. He bought music of popular singers and watched performances of the Royal Ballet and the American Ballet Theatre.

For the next few years, Soviet officials kept their eyes on Baryshnikov whenever the Kirov Ballet went on tour. Other talented dancers, such as Rudolf Nureyev and Natalia Makarova, had already defected, and the Soviets did not want to lose Baryshnikov as well. But Baryshnikov was growing restless with the Kirov Ballet and its traditional style of dancing. He wanted to experiment with new forms of dance and to perform more than his usual three or four times a month. Unlike American dancers, Kirov dancers spent most of their time in rehearsals and very little time on stage.

Baryshnikov made his last appearance as a Russian dancer on June 29, 1974. He had decided to defect, although that meant he might never see his family, friends, or homeland again. "I finally decided that if I let the opportunity of expanding my art in the West slip by, it would haunt me always," he said. "What I have done is called a crime in Russia. . . . But my life is my art and I realized it would be a greater crime to destroy that."[9]

Baryshnikov performed his first role as a "western" dancer in a Canadian television production of the ballet *La Sylphide*. His first appearance on stage after his defection took place in the United States on July 27, 1974. He performed in the American Ballet Theatre's *Giselle* to a sold-out audience. Baryshnikov received twenty-four curtain calls, and his dancing was described as "perfection" in a newspaper review.[10]

For the next four years, Baryshnikov continued performing with the American Ballet Theatre. He enthusiastically threw himself into the works of modern choreographers such as Alvin Ailey, Jerome Robbins, Twyla Tharp, Merce Cunningham, and Paul Taylor. Tharp created the dance *Push Comes to Shove* for Baryshnikov in 1976. He was so successful in that role that the American Ballet Theatre decided no other dancer would perform the lead. If Baryshnikov was injured or ill and could not dance the part, the performance would be canceled.

In 1977, Baryshnikov appeared in the movie *The Turning Point*, playing a part that reflected his own life—a Russian dancer in an American company. The film was a hit at the box office and turned Baryshnikov into a movie star as well as a ballet star. Also in 1977, Baryshnikov tried his hand at choreography by revising *The Nutcracker* ballet. A year later, he created a new *Don Quixote*.

When Baryshnikov was thirty, he decided to move from the American Ballet Theatre to the New York City Ballet, where he could work with choreographer George Balanchine. Baryshnikov wanted the challenge of Balanchine's intricate choreography and difficult footwork. "I'm afraid to get bored with something," Baryshnikov has said. "For me, that would mean the end of life."[11]

"My life is my art," says Baryshnikov, whose dancing has been described as "perfection."

Baryshnikov appeared with the New York City Ballet for the first time on July 7, 1978, in *Coppelia*. While most dancers learn two to three ballets each season, Baryshnikov learned twenty-two in his first year. He returned to the American Ballet Theatre in 1980 as its artistic director. He has been credited with bringing new life to the company through his interpretations of classical and modern dance.[12]

During his nine years as the American Ballet Theatre's director, Baryshnikov became a United

States citizen. Always eager to try something new, he decided in 1990 to start his own dance company, the White Oak Dance Project. Baryshnikov's company consists of six to twelve dancers and focuses on performing the works of modern dance choreographers who are not well known.

Regarded as the greatest dancer in the world today, Baryshnikov turned fifty in 1998. He lives in New York City with former ballerina Lisa Rinehart and their three children. He also has an older daughter who lives with her mother, the actress Jessica Lange.

Besides running the White Oak Dance Project, Baryshnikov still dances occasionally and regularly takes ballet classes. "I have no idea where I am headed," Baryshnikov has said. "And that can be scary. But to me it's also exciting."[13]

Glossary

Broadway—The major theater district of New York City, where plays and musicals are performed.

choreographer—A person who creates dances.

choreography—The art of creating dances.

corps de ballet—The dancers in a ballet company who perform as a group.

debut—A performer's first public appearance.

defect—To leave one's country for political reasons with no intention of returning.

Emmy award—An award given by the Academy of Television Arts and Sciences for outstanding achievement in television.

ensemble—A group of dancers, singers, or musicians who perform together.

lyrics—The words of a song.

lyricist—A person who writes the words to a song.

Oscar—An award given by the Academy of Motion Picture Arts and Sciences for achievement in films; also called an Academy Award.

premiere—The first public performance of a work, such as a ballet or play.

review—An article in a newspaper or magazine that evaluates a performance.

soloist—A person who performs alone.

Tony award—An award given for outstanding achievement in Broadway theater.

troupe—A company of theatrical performers.

vaudeville—A variety of musical entertainment acts on stage, including acrobats, comedians, singers, dancers, and even performing animals.

Chapter Notes

All magazine articles were obtained from InfoTrac, a database of periodicals from the Information Access Corporation. InfoTrac is available at most libraries.

Preface

1. Mikhail Baryshnikov, *Baryshnikov at Work* (New York: Alfred A. Knopf, 1980), p. 10.

2. Aljean Harmetz, "Astaire, Nearing 80, Is Still a Very Private Person," *The New York Times*, May 8, 1979, p. C9.

3. "Robbins, the Legend Who Was Human," *The New York Times*, August 9, 1998, sec. 2, p. 26.

4. Twyla Tharp, *Push Comes to Shove* (New York: Bantam Books, 1992), p. 9.

5. Allen Robertson and Donald Hutera, *The Dance Handbook* (London: England: Longman Group UK, Limited, 1988), p. 134.

6. Robert Coe, *Dance in America* (New York: E. P. Dutton, 1985), p. 213.

7. Tharp, p. 106.

Chapter 1. Martha Graham

1. Martha Graham, *Blood Memory* (New York: Doubleday, 1991), p. 19.

2. Terry Teachout, "Martha Graham," *Time 100 Poll*, http://www.pathfinder.com/time/time100/artists/profile/graham.html.

3. Graham, p. 39.

4. Agnes de Mille, *Martha: The Life and Work of Martha Graham* (New York: Random House, 1956, 1991), p. 21.

5. Don McDonagh, *Martha Graham: A Biography* (New York: Praeger, 1973), p. 25.

6. Jane Sherman and Norton Owen, "Martha Graham and Ted Shawn," *Dance Magazine*, July 1995, p. 42.

7. Ernestine Stodelle, *Deep Song: The Dance Story of Martha Graham* (New York: Schirmer Books, 1984), p. 32.

8. Graham, p. 103.

9. Dolores Barclay, "Martha Graham and the Hidden Language of the Soul," *Associated Press*, April 1, 1991.

10. Graham, p. 110.

11. Ibid., p. 202.

12. Linda Winer, "Limelight: Drawing Energy from a Legend," *Newsday*, April 5, 1991, p. 67.

13. Leroy Leatherman, *Martha Graham: Portrait of the Lady as an Artist* (New York: Alfred A. Knopf, 1966), p. 32.

14. Winer, p. 67.

Chapter 2. Fred Astaire

1. Fred Astaire, *Steps in Time* (New York: Harper & Brothers, 1959), p. 14.

2. Ibid., p. 20.

3. Bob Thomas, *Astaire: The Man, The Dancer* (New York: St. Martin's Press, 1984), p. 19.

4. Fred Bruning, "Fred Astaire, Hollywood's Top Song-and-Dance Man, Dies at 88," *Newsday*, June 23, 1987, p. 5.

5. Ibid.

6. Aljean Harmetz, "Astaire, Nearing 80, Is Still a Very Private Person," *The New York Times*, May 8, 1979, p. C9.

7. Betty Lasky, RKO: *The Biggest Little Major of Them All* (Englewood Cliffs, N.J.: Prentice-Hall, 1984), p. 99.

8. Bruning, p. 5.

9. Richard De Atley, "From Flunked Screen Test to America's Greatest Dancer," *Associated Press*, June 23, 1987.

10. John Mueller, *Astaire Dancing* (New York: Alfred A. Knopf, 1985), p. 8.

11. Anna Kisselgoff, "Fred Astaire Perfected a New Art Form," *The New York Times*, June 28, 1987, p. H20.

12. Brad Darrach, "He Made Us Feel Like Dancing," *People Weekly*, July 6, 1987, p. 96.

13. Stanley Green and Burt Goldblatt, *Starring Fred Astaire* (New York: Dodd, Mead & Company, 1973), p. 4.

14. Bruning, p. 5.

15. Astaire, p. 325.

Chapter 3: George Balanchine

1. Bernard Taper, *Balanchine, a Biography* (New York: Times Books, 1984), p. 128.

2. Valerie Scher, "George Balanchine, the Symbol of Modern Ballet Choreography," *The Philadelphia Inquirer*, May 1, 1983, p. D8.

3. Francis Mason, *I Remember Balanchine* (New York: Doubleday, 1991), p. xi.

4. John Gruen, "Tamara Geva, First a Muse and Then a Wife," *Dance Magazine*, June 1997, p. 104–108.

5. Anna Kisselgoff, "George Balanchine, 79, Dies in New York," *The New York Times*, May 1, 1983, p. A1.

6. Taper, p. 76.

7. Ibid., p. 121.

8. Jennifer Dunning, *"But First a School"* (New York: Viking, 1985), p. 14.

9. Clive Barnes, "The Great Dance Way," *Dance Magazine*, August 1996, pp. 98–101.

10. Lincoln Kirstein, *The New York City Ballet* (New York: Alfred A. Knopf, 1973), p. 206.

11. Scher, p. D8.

12. Linda Doeser, *Ballet and Dance* (New York: St. Martin's Press, 1977), p. 17.

13. Michael Walsh, "The Joy of Pure Movement," *Time*, May 9, 1983, p. 91.

14. Kisselgoff, p. A1.

Chapter 4. Agnes de Mille

1. Agnes de Mille, *Dance to the Piper* (Boston: Little, Brown and Company, 1951), p. 305.

2. Ibid.

3. Agnes de Mille, *Where the Wings Grow* (New York: Doubleday & Company, 1978), p. 76.

4. Ibid., p. 79.

5. De Mille, *Dance to the Piper*, p. 42.

6. Carol Easton, *No Intermissions: The Life of Agnes de Mille* (Boston: Little, Brown and Company, 1996), p. 33.

7. De Mille, *Dance to the Piper*, p. 99.

8. *Agnes: The Indomitable de Mille*, videotape documentary, Great Performances/Dance in America, WNET, New York, 1987.

9. Jess Gregg, "Eaten Alive: A Writer's Casual Encounter in a Coffee Shop Led to a Warm Friendship with the Irascible Agnes de Mille," *Dance Magazine*, January 1998, p. 60.

10. De Mille, *Dance to the Piper*, p. 304.

11. Max Wilk, *OK! The Story of Oklahoma!* (New York: Grove Press, 1993), p. 150.

12. Anna Kisselgoff, "Dance View: An Artist Who Spoke for the People," *The New York Times*, October 17, 1993, sec. 2, p. 10.

13. Easton, p. 278.

14. Agnes de Mille, *Reprieve: A Memoir* (New York: Doubleday & Company, 1981), p. 69.

Chapter 5. Katherine Dunham

1. Katherine Dunham, *A Touch of Innocence* (New York: Harcourt, Brace and Company, 1959), p. 54.

2. Jack Anderson, "The Ailey Stages Works by Katherine Dunham," *The New York Times*, December 24, 1988, p. 17.

3. Dunham, p. 55.

4. Ibid., p. 66.

5. Ibid., p. 104.

6. Paula Durbin, "The First Lady of Caribbean Cadences," *Americas*, January–February 1996, p. 36.

7. Bebe Moore Campbell, "The 1990 Essence Awards," *Essence*, October 1990, p. 55.

8. Durbin, p. 36.

9. Katherine Dunham, *Katherine Dunham's Journey to Accompong* (Westport, Conn.: Negro Universities Press, 1971), p. 135.

10. Agnes de Mille, *Portrait Gallery* (Boston: Houghton Mifflin Company, 1990), p. 49.

11. Durbin, p. 36.

12. Paul Ben-Itzak, "Dunham Legacy Stands at Risk," *Dance Magazine*, January 1995, p. 40.

13. Jennifer Dunning, "A Katherine Dunham Celebration," *The New York Times*, January 14, 1979, sec. 2, p. 14.

14. Elizabeth Gleick, "Hunger Strike: Dance Legend Katherine Dunham Ends Her Fast for the People of Haiti," *People Weekly*, March 30, 1992, p. 42.

15. Robert Cohan, *The Dance Workshop* (New York: Simon & Schuster, 1986), p. 154.

16. Campbell, p. 55.

Chapter 6. Jerome Robbins

1. "The Right Moves," *People Weekly*, August 17, 1998, p. 106.

2. Richard Corliss, "Peter Pan Flies Again; Dance Master Jerome Robbins Returns Triumphantly to Broadway," *Time*, March 6, 1989, p. 78.

3. Anna Kisselgoff, "Jerome Robbins, 79, Is Dead: Giant of Ballet and Broadway," *The New York Times*, July 30, 1998, p. A1.

4. Nancy Goldner, "Choreographer Jerome Robbins Is Dead at 79," *The Philadelphia Inquirer*, July 30, 1998, p. A1.

5. *People Weekly*, p. 106.

6. Corliss, p. 78.

7. Terry Teachout, "Choreography by Jerome Robbins," *Commentary*, April 1997, p. 58.

8. Richard Natale, "Jerome Robbins," *Variety*, August 3, 1998, p. 47.

9. Teachout, p. 58.

10. Marilyn Hunt, "Robbins Speaks!" *Dance Magazine*, September 1997, p. 27.

11. Gerald M. Berkowitz, *New Broadways: Theatre Across America as the Millennium Approaches* (New York: Applause, 1997), pp. 205–206.

12. Terry Teachout, "A 'Made in the U.S.A.' Genius: Jerome Robbins, Master Choreographer," *Time*, August 10, 1998, p. 82.

13. Teachout, "Choreography by Jerome Robbins," p. 58.

14. "Robbins, the Legend Who Was Human," *The New York Times*, August 9, 1998, sec. 2, p. 26.

15. Ibid.

Chapter 7. Bob Fosse

1. Kevin Boyd Grubb, *Razzle Dazzle: The Life and Work of Bob Fosse* (New York: St. Martin's Press, 1989), p. 6.

2. Ibid., p. 8.

3. Ibid., p. 13.

4. Ibid., p. 28.

5. Martin Gottfried, *All His Jazz: The Life and Death of Bob Fosse* (New York: Bantam Books, 1990), p. 81.

6. William B. Collins, "Fosse's Legacy: All That Dance," *The Philadelphia Inquirer*, September 25, 1987, p. D1.

7. Jeremy Gerard, "Bob Fosse, a Stylish 'Original,' Is Remembered by His Peers," *The New York Times*, September 25, 1987, p. D16.

8. Barry Rehfeld, "Fosse's Follies: The Man Who Brought You 'All That Jazz' and 'Cabaret' Presents 'Star 80,' His Latest Tour of the Seamy Side of the Streets Paved with Gold," *Rolling Stone*, January 19, 1984, pp. 42–45.

9. "Life Was a Cabaret to Bob Fosse—Dancer, Director and One of a Kind," *People Weekly*, October 12, 1987, pp. 87–91.

10. Rehfeld, pp. 42–45.

11. Richard Maltby, Jr., "Hot Moves in Honor of a Maverick," *Maclean's*, August 24, 1998, pp. 48–51.

12. Eileen Putnam, "Bob Fosse, the Choreographer and Director Whose Genius Spawned Such Broadway Musicals as 'Sweet Charity' and 'Dancin' as well as the Film Version of 'Cabaret' Is Dead at Age 60," *Associated Press*, September 24, 1987.

Chapter 8. Alvin Ailey

1. Jennifer Dunning, *Alvin Ailey: A Life in Dance* (Reading, Mass.: Addison-Wesley, 1996), p. 35.

2. Alvin Ailey, *Revelations: The Autobiography of Alvin Ailey* (New York: Carol Publishing Group, 1995), pp. 40–41.

3. Joseph H. Mazo, *Prime Movers* (New York: William Morrow and Company, Inc., 1977), p. 256.

4. Ailey, p. 18.

5. Dunning, p. 9.

6. Barbara Rosen, "Giant of Modern Dance Dies at 58," *Associated Press*, December 2, 1989.

7. Jennifer Dunning, "Alvin Ailey, a Leading Figure in Modern Dance, Dies at 58," *The New York Times*, December 2, 1989, p. A1.

8. Nancy Goldner, "Dance's Alvin Ailey Dead at 58," *The Philadelphia Inquirer*, December 2, 1989, p. A1.

9. Ailey, p. 89.

10. "With Dances Deeply Rooted in His Personal Heritage, Choreographer Alvin Ailey Touched Millions," *People Weekly*, December 18, 1989, p. 166.

11. Janice Berman, "Renowned Choreographer Alvin Ailey Is Dead at 58," *Newsday*, December 2, 1989, p. 2.

12. Dunning, "Alvin Ailey, a Leading Figure in Modern Dance, Dies at 58," p. A1.

13. Anna Kisselgoff, "Ailey: Dancing the Dream," *The New York Times*, December 4, 1988, p. H1.

14. Bill Stieg, "Dancer, Choreographer Remembered," *Associated Press*, December 9, 1989.

Chapter 9. Twyla Tharp

1. Twyla Tharp, *Push Comes to Shove* (New York: Bantam Books, 1992), p. 79.
2. Ibid., p. 83.
3. Pam Lambert, "Push Comes to Shove: Book Review," *People Weekly*, March 15, 1993, p. 32.
4. Tharp, p. 6.
5. Ibid., p. 9.
6. Ibid., p. 30.
7. Elizabeth Zimmer, "Memoir in Motion," *Harper's Bazaar*, December 1992, p. 66.
8. Tharp, p. 49.
9. Robert Coe, *Dance in America* (New York: E. P. Dutton, 1985), p. 213.
10. Linda Doeser, *Ballet and Dance* (New York: St. Martin's Press, 1977), p. 64.
11. Coe, p. 214.
12. Ellen Switzer, *Dancers! Horizons in American Dance* (New York: Atheneum, 1982), p. 119.
13. Martha Duffy, "Tharp Moves Out from Wingside; Her New Ballets Show a Masterly Range of Choreographic Skill," *Time*, February 13, 1984, p. 52.
14. Arlene Croce, "Twyla Tharp Looks Ahead and Thinks Back," *The New Yorker*, January 23, 1995, p. 30.
15. *Associated Press*, October 26, 1997.
16. Tharp, p. 106.
17. Holly Brubach, "Twyla Tharp's Return," *The Atlantic*, March 1987, p. 86.
18. *Associated Press*, October 26, 1997.

Chapter 10. Mikhail Baryshnikov

1. Jim Jerome, "A Bold Leap for Misha," *People Weekly*, December 16, 1985, p. 152.
2. Barbara Aria, *Misha: The Mikhail Baryshnikov Story* (New York: St. Martin's Press, 1989), p. 15.

3. Anna Kisselgoff, "Baryshnikov Cites Soviet Curb on Art," *The New York Times,* July 23, 1974, p. A30.

4. Gennady Smakov, *Baryshnikov: From Russia to the West* (New York: Farrar, Straus and Giroux, 1981), p. 16.

5. Mikhail Baryshnikov, *Baryshnikov at Work* (New York: Alfred A. Knopf, 1980), p. 10.

6. Aria, p. 20.

7. Baryshnikov, p. 8.

8. Aria, p. 48.

9. "Baryshnikov, Defecting Dancer, Says Decision Was Not Political," *Associated Press,* July 6, 1974.

10. John Rockwell, "Conservatively, Baryshnikov is Overwhelming," *The New York Times,* August 4, 1974, sec. 2, p. 1.

11. Eric Levin, "Turning Point: Having Abruptly Quit the American Ballet Theatre, Mikhail Baryshnikov Is a Man Without a Company. He May Be Happier That Way." *Life,* November 1989, p. 50.

12. "How Russian Emigres Are Shaping U.S. Culture," *U.S. News & World Report,* March 28, 1983, p. 35.

13. Levin, p. 50.

Further Reading

De Mille, Agnes. *Portrait Gallery*. Boston: Houghton Mifflin Company, 1990.

De Mille, Agnes. *Where the Wings Grow*. New York: Doubleday & Company, Inc., 1978.

Dominy, Jeannine. *Katherine Dunham*. New York: Chelsea House Publishers, 1992.

Freedman, Russell. *Martha Graham, a Dancer's Life*. New York: Clarion Books, 1998.

Goodman, Saul. *Baryshnikov, a Most Spectacular Dancer*. New York: Harvey House, 1979.

Krista, Davida. *George Balanchine: American Ballet Master*. Minneapolis: Lerner Publications Co., 1996.

Lewis-Ferguson, Julinda. *Alvin Ailey, Jr.: A Life in Dance*. New York: Walker, 1994.

Mueller, John. *Astaire Dancing: The Musical Films*. New York: Alfred A. Knopf, 1985.

Internet Addresses

Alvin Ailey:
<http://www.alvinailey.org/>

Fred Astaire (this site includes excellent photographs of Astaire from childhood through adulthood):
<http://www.fredastaire.net/>

George Balanchine:
<http://www.nycballet.com/about/nycbgbbio.html>

Agnes de Mille:
<http://kennedy-center.org/calendar/index.cfm?fuseaction=showIndividual&entitY_id=3719&source_type=A>

Katherine Dunham:
> <http://kennedy-center.org/calendar/
> index.cfm?fuseaction=showIndividual&entitY_id=
> 3721&source_type=A>

Bob Fosse:
> <http://www.fosse.com>

Martha Graham:
> <http://www.time.com/time/time100/artists/profile/
> graham.html>

Jerome Robbins:
> <http://www.flash.net/~actor./jerome.htm>

Twyla Tharp:
> <http://www.achievement.org/autodoc/page/
> tha0bio-1>

This History of Dance page contains information on the roots of many categories of dance along with lists of dance studios and competitions by state:
> <http://www.centralhome.com/ballroomcountry/
> history.htm>

Brief biographical sketches of nearly 150 choreographers for the American Ballet Theatre. Click on the "view by choreographers" tab at the top of the page:
> <http://www.abt.org/education/archive/index.html>

A listing of national and international ballet companies:
> <http://dir.yahoo.com/Arts/Performing_Arts/Dance/
> Ballet/Ballet_Companies>

A listing of modern dance companies:
> <http://dir.yahoo.com/Arts/Performing_Arts/Dance/
> Modern/Modern_Companies>

Index

A

Ailey, Alvin, 4, 6, **72**, 73–77,
 78, 79
 contribution to dance, 73,
  76–77, 79
 Revelations, 6, 76
Alvin Ailey American Dance
 Theater, 76-79
American Ballet, 32
American Ballet Theatre, 43,
 58, 77, 88, 95-97
Astaire, Adele, 17–21
Astaire, Fred, 4–6, **16**, 17–21,
 22, 23–24
 contribution to dance, 5, 17,
  21, 23–24
 Rogers, Ginger, perfor-
  mances with, 21, **22**, 23
 Top Hat, 21

B

Balanchine, George, 4, 6, 25,
 26, 27–30, **31**, 32–34, 50,
 56, 59, 60, 62, 96
 contribution to dance, 25,
  30, 33-34
 New York City Ballet, and
  the, 30, 32–33
 Slaughter on Tenth Avenue,
  32
Ballet Negre, 48
Ballet Russe de Monte Carlo,
 40, 74
Ballet Society, 32
Ballet Theatre. *See* American
 Ballet Theatre
Ballets Russes, 29
Baryshnikov, Mikhail, 4–6, 86,
 90, 91–96, **97**, 98
 contribution to dance, 5, 98
Bernstein, Leonard, 58, 77
Bolshoi Ballet, 91
British Royal Ballet, 88, 95

C

Coccia, Aurelia, 20
Copland, Aaron, 13, 40
Cunningham, Merce, 5, 15, 85,
 96

D

Dance Theater of Harlem, 77
de Lavallade, Carmen, 74-75
de Mille, Agnes, 4–6, 32,
 35–36, **37**, 38–41, **42**, 43
 contribution to dance, 5,
  40–41, 43
 Oklahoma!, 6, 40-41
 Rodeo, 35, **37**, 40
De Mille, Cecil B., 36
Denishawn, 10, 12
Diaghilev, Serge, 29-30
Dunham, Katherine, 5–6, 44,
 45, 46–50, **51**, 52–53, 71,
 73–74, 76
 contribution to dance, 5, 46,
  50, 52–53

E

Eastman School of Dance, 11

F

Fosse, Bob, 4, 6, 63–64, **65**,
 66–70
 Cabaret, 69
 contribution to dance, 63,
  70
 Sweet Charity, **69**

G

Godunov, Alexander, 92–93

Graham, Martha, 5, 7, **8**, 9–13,
    14, 15, 41, 75, 85
    Appalachian Spring, 13
    contribution to dance, 5, 7,
        12, 15
Grass, Charles, 64, 67

H
Hammerstein, Oscar II, 40
Hawkins, Erick, 13
Holm, Hanya, 75
Horton, Lester, 74-75

I
Imperial Ballet Company, 28

J
Jamison, Judith, 79
Joffrey Ballet, 77, 86
Joyner-Kersee, Jackie, 52

K
Katherine Dunham Dancers,
    50, 52–53, 71, 73–74
Kelly, Gene, 70–71
Kirov Ballet, 93–95
Kirstein, Lincoln, 30, 32

L
Limón, José, 67
Loring, Eugene, 58

M
Makarova, Natalia, 95
Martins, Peter, 62, 88
Metropolitan Opera, 32
Mitchell, Arthur, 5

N
New York City Ballet, 59–62,
    96–97. *See also* Balanchine,
    George
Nureyev, Rudolf, 95

P
Paris Opera Ballet, 30, 77, 88

Pavlova, Anna, 38
Pushkin, Alexander, 93

R
Robbins, Jerome, 5–6, 32, 34,
    54, 55–58, **59**, 60–62,
    67–68, 85, 96
    contribution to dance, 6, 55,
        57–60, 62
    Fancy Free, 58, **59**
    West Side Story, 6, 59–61
Robinson, Bill "Bojangles," 5,
    66
Rodgers, Richard, 40
Royal Danish Ballet, 30

S
St. Denis, Ruth, 5, 10
Sandor, Gluck, 56–57
School of American Ballet, 30,
    56
Shawn, Ted, 5, 10–11, 76
Sokolow, Anna, 67
Stravinsky, Igor, 33

T
Tallchief, Maria, 5, 33
Taylor, Paul, 15, 85, 96
Tharp, Twyla, 6, 15, **80**, 81–86,
    87, 88–89, 96
    contribution to dance, 82,
        86, 89
    Push Comes to Shove, 86
Tudor, Antony, 58

V
vaudeville, 18-19, 23, 46,
    63–64

W
Weaver, Frederic, 64
Weidman, Charles, 75
White Oak Dance Project, 98